MODELLING
German World War II
Armoured Vehicles

MODELLING
German World War II Armoured Vehicles

Robin Buckland

THE CROWOOD PRESS

First published in 2019 by
The Crowood Press Ltd
Ramsbury, Marlborough
Wiltshire SN8 2HR

www.crowood.com

British Library Cataloguing-in-Publication Data
A catalogue record for this book is available from the British Library.

ISBN 978 1 78500 515 2

Designed and typeset by Guy Croton Publishing Services,
West Malling, Kent

Printed and bound in India by Replika Press Pvt Ltd

Contents

Chapter One

Introduction

From the time when I started making military vehicle models back in the 1960s, there has been a continued and significant interest in building German equipment, from World War II in particular. Back in those days, there was only a limited variety of models on the market, with the leader being the range of smaller 1/76 scale kits by Airfix. In the years since then, so much has changed and the market today is a modeller's paradise compared to what is was like some fifty years ago. We have seen manufacturers come and go, though have also been fortunate that most of the kits from those we have lost have been taken on by others and are still regularly produced. However, it is not practical to keep all of the kits in a range in continual production, especially for the long-established brands where their product catalogue has grown so much over the years, so kits may have to be scheduled for production runs over time. This not only applies to the big plastic kit manufacturers, but also the small resin kit producers. With resin, the rubber moulds wear out relatively quickly, so new moulds may have to be produced. This then opens the question of demand and the time that takes to build up, so kits may be unavailable for some time.

Therefore if you want a kit that is perhaps not available through the manufacturers and their distributors, keep an eye out for what is available through second-hand kit dealers, or perhaps on the bring-and-buy tables at the various model shows around the country. The other option is to wait until the manufacturer does a new production run. I have known one or two over the years that have been advertised as 'rare' for extortionate prices, only to find that the kit comes back on the market at its normal price a few months later. Tamiya's LRDG truck is one example from one of the major kit manufacturers that comes to mind.

The other thing that I think is worth saying is that when I started, those early Airfix kits were on sale at genuinely 'pocket money' prices, so youngsters (as I was then!) could afford them and get into the hobby. Many kits these days are priced way too high for youngsters (or for their parents to buy them for them), as over the years the adult model-maker has asked for more detail and the manufacturers have answered those calls, recognizing that their market is more the adult modeller, so prices have risen accordingly. Obviously that is not the entire story and there are some kits which can be used to encourage the younger modeller. I am a keen supporter of anything that will encourage new modellers to get into our hobby and perhaps away from computer screens for a while.

One of the most important advances in modelling has been as a result of the collapse of the Berlin Wall and the end of the Warsaw Pact. The opening up of Eastern Europe saw the emergence of a host of new information that was accessible to all. One of the most notable results was the information that I think came first from David Fletcher, the well-known armour historian who worked at the Tank Museum in Bovington, and his trip to the Russian armour collection at Kubinka, when it emerged that contrary to previous information, an example of the huge German Maus had survived the war.

Another major advance has been due to the rapid development of the computer. It's hard to think of life without them these days, but I for

*Nearly 50 years old, my Jagdpanther conversion based on the Airfix Panther chassis.
Not brilliant but it was good enough for me back then.*

one had already left school before IBM made its first personal computer, which went on the market back in 1982. For modellers, the use of computer-controlled mould-making machines has reduced the time needed to make new moulds; couple that to laser-cut moulds, it means that kit manufacturers can now provide accurate moulds that take a fraction of the time and cost to create. Most recently, though not quite a household item yet, the use of 3D printers will I am sure make even more of an impact in the next few years, as their quality goes up and their cost comes down. We might talk of scratch-building or using plasticard to build new parts for a conversion, but while I did that for many years, nowadays I find it more efficient to utilize the many kits and conversion sets that are commercially available. I know some

will still choose to scratch-build, but it tends to be only a minority of skilled modellers who have the time and inclination to go down that route.

In the 1960s, the only small-scale tank kits available were the old Airfix ones. They did quite a neat StuG III, but the turreted Pz III was not available until ESCI appeared on the scene with a couple of 1/72 scale models and Matchbox (now Revell) produced the Ausf L (*Ausführen*: version). So if you wanted a Pz III gun tank, you had no option but to carry out a conversion on the Airfix kit, scratch-building the turret itself. Built when I was still a young teenager, mine was nowhere near as good as the modern kits, but at the time I was happy with it because I did at least have a Pz III in my collection. I also created a Jagdpanther based on the old Airfix Panther.

My surviving example of the early SdKfz 251 in polyester resin by Eric Clarke.

Back in the 1970s and 1980s, due to the pressure of costs and an international oil crisis, the rate of new kit releases slowed to a trickle. At that point, we saw the growth of what we have come to call 'cottage industries'. Some skilled modellers would scratch-build their own model based on a set of scale drawings, and from that 'master' they could make a mould and then sell castings of it. These could be moulded in metal or a two-part resin. The very early models by Eric Clark (which evolved into Milicast, the creators of a huge range of polyurethane models today) were done in a polyester resin, which could not manage finer details such as axles and gun barrels. Then new polyurethane resins became available and suddenly a whole new level of detail became possible. The likes of Alain Lafarge in France with his AL-BY models and then Cromwell Models with their modern IDF Merkava I introduced us to the detail possible with the then new polyurethane resin, a material which has since gone from strength to strength. We have also seen a few manufacturers produce models in white metal, with some excellent detail, such as those by MMS and SHQ.

Another modelling revolution was the emergence of the 1/35 armour model, whose development was due to the work of companies such as Tamiya, since followed by others like Dragon Models and Trumpeter, who have grown their ranges to sizes and with subjects that modellers once would have only dreamt of. The sheer variety of what is available on the market these days is amazing. As a modeller in my sixties now, there are plastic kits available of subjects that I never imagined I would see when I was younger. When I began, I found it difficult to get examples of simply the Panzer I through to VI. Now I can not only buy all of them, but each version of each one, even the prototypes! Going back to those early days, I still have one of the first 1/35 scale (roughly) kits that I built. I can't recall the manufacturer (though I think it may have been Nitto), and it is an SdKfz (Sonderkraftfahrzeug) 222, which even has a wind-up clockwork motor. Over forty years later it is still in one of my storage drawers, a little battered with one or two small parts broken off, but generally still all there. Now, where did I put that key …?

Clockwork SdKfz 222.

Clockwork winder hidden underneath.

The Internet has also had an impact on the model-maker – you can judge for yourself that we have seen a huge reduction in the number of model shops on the high street and are also seeing the sales of paper-based hobby magazines suffering. People shop via the Internet and look around web shops to get the best deals they can; even if the kits are being shipped from abroad, they can check stock, get the best price, pay online and then wait for the order to appear via the post or one of the many courier services. Many people rely on the Internet these days for their information and very often simply expect it to be free. Something for free is nice, but the reality is that people need to earn a living from what they do, or that information you want will not be written in the first place. But change is inevitable and continual, so we will just have to see how the future works out. In the meantime, let's make sure we continue to enjoy our model-making hobby.

THE PZKPFW I

This light tank was the first of the new Panzers for the Wehrmacht built in the 1930s. It was really intended more as a training vehicle that would also enable the armament manufacturers to get some practice in making armoured vehicles after the ban imposed by the Versailles Treaty was discarded. Armed with just two 7.92mm machine guns, it could do little more than provide some infantry support. The design of the suspension was influenced by the British Carden Lloyd designs of the same period. Over 1,100 examples of the Ausf A were built, which are identified by the trailing idler wheel that runs on the ground. It had some issues and a slightly longer Ausf B was made, which is identified quickly by an extra road wheel along with an external beam, and the rear idler is raised up off the ground. Around 400 of the Ausf B were built as turreted tanks and additional chassis were built as Command vehicles (Panzerbefehlswagen). Turretless ones were used as driver training machines.

Two later variants, the Ausf C and the Ausf F, were built later, though only in small numbers. They bore no resemblance to the earlier versions and were intended as heavily armoured reconnaissance machines, but still only armed with machine guns.

The chassis of the Ausf B was used to build the first tank hunters (Panzerjäger), and were armed with a Czech 4.7cm anti-tank gun in a fixed shield mounting. The Ausf B chassis was also used for an early self-propelled artillery piece, where the turret and superstructure were removed and a large boxed gun shield, open on top and at the back, plus a 15cm sIG33 (schwere Infanterie Geschütze: heavy infantry gun) was fitted, complete with full carriage including the wheels. Used by six Panzer divisions during the Blitzkrieg of 1940, a number were still in service with 5th Panzer Division in Russia as late as 1943. Other variants used in small numbers include a Demolition charge-laying tank, the Ladungsleger, which was built in two versions, both with cable-operated arms to lay the 50kg charge, one which laid it ahead of the tank and another which simply let it drop behind it. A few Pz I Ausf A were converted into flamethrowers by the engineer team of 5th Pz Division in North Africa, with the flame projector replacing the right-hand turret machine gun. These were done in readiness for the assault on Tobruk.

In the later stages of the war, no longer suitable for use in front-line combat, the tanks had their turrets removed and replaced by a large box to be used as an ammunition or load carrier. The turrets were not entirely wasted, as they were installed in various permanent fortifications. By May 1944, records indicate that 511 of the available turrets had been released for this purpose. Coupled with the use of the Pz I as a driver training vehicle in basic training for Panzer crews, a design that was quickly found to be obsolete for front-line service proved to be a useful resource for the Wehrmacht well into the war.

Chapter Two

Historical Background

WORLD WAR I

In World War I, the development of the tank was in the hands of both the British and the French. Those early machines were the chosen solution to the stalemate of trench warfare that developed on the Western Front in the early years of the war. Artillery and the machine gun were changing the face of modern warfare and the vast number of casualties demonstrated a desperate need to find a new answer. The tank, an armoured, mobile box that could traverse open ground and crush

The replica A7V at the Tank Museum, Bovington.

This is the box art for a recent 1/35 kit of the A7V, including the interior detail fittings.

extensive barbed wire entanglements while providing protection for the crew inside, provided part of the solution. Tanks, in turn, carried machine guns or artillery to bring fire to bear on the enemy trenches and emplacements as they got closer to them. The early British and French tanks were built in large numbers. The German army made use of captured examples, but only designed one tank of its own, the A7V, and only twenty of those were built in total. Just one of these rare tanks, Mephisto, has survived to this day and is now to be found in a museum in Australia, although a few years ago a full-size wooden replica was built and is now displayed in the collection of the Tank Museum, Bovington.

Coming late in the war, two prototype examples of the Leichter Kampfwagen II (LE.II) were built, armed only with machine guns and looking similar in layout to the British Whippet. A few were built after the end of the war for Sweden. Germany did also make a number of armoured cars, but these did not see significant service during the war.

With the war over, the Treaty of Verseilles prohibited Germany from possessing either tanks or aircraft within the limited armed forces the country was allowed to retain. But they managed to circumvent the prohibition, even before Hitler came to power. A secret tank training school was set up in Russia, the Kama Training school, located in Kazan and opening in 1929. A number of German officers underwent training in armoured warfare, using tanks provided by the Soviets. There were about a dozen officers at any one time, attending a two-year course. Commanders such as Heinz Guderian and Walter Model were among those early trainees. The situation moved on, however, when Hitler came to power and German rearmament was openly pursued. The school closed in late 1933.

THE 1930S AND THE SPANISH CIVIL WAR

After Hitler's rise to power in 1933, a civil war in Spain turned out to be a proving ground for the newer elements of the German armed forces, both aircraft and tanks. The Condor Legion supported the Spanish Nationalist movement of General Franco. In addition to the well-known involvement of many new aircraft types, there were also ground troops and a number of the Panzer I light tank. The Panzer I was only armed with machine guns, however, and was inferior to the Russian-built T-26 that it usually faced in Spain. Nevertheless, it gave the German crews valuable experience in working together in combat operations, alongside ground troops.

The 1930s also saw the development of the slightly larger Panzer II, which was fitted with a 20mm main gun, alongside an mg. The other 'fashion' of tank design in the 1930s was the multi-turreted heavy tank. A lot of money and effort was put into these by a number of countries. In Russia, both the T-28 and the even bigger T-35 were built. The UK built the Independent, though only in prototype form. France developed the large Char 2C, while Germany built a few mild steel prototypes of the Neubaufahrzeug, to which I will return in a moment.

EARLY WORLD WAR II

By 1939, the most numerous tanks in service with the Wehrmacht were the Pz I and the Pz II, plus a small number of the early variants of the Pz III and Pz IV medium tanks. After the occupation of Czechoslovakia, the Wehrmacht also absorbed both the Pz 35(t) and Pz 38(t) tanks, which were added to their inventory for the subsequent Blitzkrieg assault of France and the Low Countries in May 1940.

There was also one other tank design used at this time, though only in very small numbers and only the mild steel prototype rather than the fully armoured production version. This was the Neubaufahrzeug, a multi-turreted design that was deployed briefly in the invasion of Norway. The key to the success of the Panzers during these Blitzkrieg operations lay not so much in the power of the tank, but the combination of tactics, which involved the concentration of the tank units, the speed at which they moved, the close support of mobile artillery and the assistance of Luftwaffe close-support aircraft.

The French tank force possessed far more tanks than the Wehrmacht, with the majority of them also being better armed. The tanks in operation with the British Expeditionary Force were armed with mostly just two-pounder main guns, or, in the case of the Matilda I, just a single machine gun. Despite that, the sheer volume of captured enemy equipment was something of a windfall to the German military and many of the French tanks in particular were to resurface as mounts for self-propelled anti-tank guns and artillery, appearing in North Africa, Russia, Italy and later Normandy.

Following the fall of France, and due in part to his ally Mussolini's territorial ambitions, Hitler's Germany was pulled into new operational areas in North Africa and the Balkans/Greece. These were followed in 1941 by the invasion of Russia. As with the invasion of France, the invasion of Russia began with quick victories and huge numbers of troops and tanks being captured. It highlighted the weakness of the older Russian designs, such as the T-26 and BT-5/7, along with the heavy, multi-turreted tank designs of the T-28 and T-35. They were knocked out in large numbers. The surprise that awaited the Panzers, however, was the new design of the T-34/76. This prompted significant changes in German tank designs.

This T-34/76, originally from Finland and now at Bovington, was the tank that had a significant impact on German tank design, leading to the Panther.

LATE WORLD WAR II

Lessons learnt in the first half of the war were calling for improved tank designs and larger guns. This meant that many of the earlier tanks were effectively obsolete, because it was not possible to fit heavier guns into the limited size turret rings of the existing hulls. Only the Pz IV was to remain in production throughout the war as a gun tank, and even that went through a number of developments. The new designs were the Tiger I, the Panther, and then the even bigger Tiger II. But what did the Germans do with all those older and captured hulls?

Many were converted to other uses. I suspect the most famous of all was the Sturmgeschütz (StuG) III, no turret and a 75mm long-barrelled gun fitted in a fixed superstructure, with quite a low profile. There were other instances of converting tanks for similar assault guns and Jagdpanzers ('Tank Hunters'), such as the StuG IV, the Marder series of anti-tank guns fitted on to the Pz 38(t)

hull, the small and agile Hetzer also based on the Pz 38(t) chassis, along with a variety of anti-tank guns and artillery pieces fitted to a number of French tank hulls captured when France was invaded. These are best known for being used by the German 21st Panzer Division in Normandy, though many were used in North Africa, Russia and Italy.

It was the second half of the war that saw the introduction of the Panther (the Panzer V) and the Tiger I, which became among the best and most famous designs of the war. The Tiger I and the even larger Tiger II were amongst the heaviest tanks to see combat during the war. The reputation of the Tiger remains to this day and the sight of Tiger 131 moving in the arena at Tiger Days or Tankfests is still a huge draw for visitors from around the world. Many World War II unit histories and diaries record reports of seeing enemy 'Tigers', even when none are now known to have been in the area. It does suggest that

This photo shows the 1/35 kit in the Cyber-Hobby range by Dragon, showing Michael Wittman's final Tiger I Befehlswagen. DRAGON MODELS

when reading some memoirs one needs to be a little careful in interpreting comments, but it also shows the effect of just the thought of being up against a Tiger.

1946 DESIGNS

A number of plans were on the drawing boards of the German arms manufacturers at end of the war. These designs utilized many common elements, which would have speeded up production, but very few reached the prototype stage. The best known of these were the E100 (just one chassis built) and the super heavy tank, Maus (two built, both knocked out in the final stages of the war). The E100 chassis was brought to the UK at the end of the war, but sadly scrapped in the 1950s. For many years it was thought that both Maus prototypes had been destroyed, but with the collapse of the Warsaw Pact and the end of the Cold War, it was discovered that the Russians had kept what appeared to be the chassis of one and the turret of the other, and combined them into one complete example, which is held in the collection at Kubinka. The remaining designs, as they were not built, are commonly referred to as 'Paper Panzers', a topic to which we will return later.

The battered prototype Schmalturm turret that would have been fitted to the Panther II design on display at Bovington. It was recovered from ranges where it had been used as a 'hard target'.

KEY TANK DESIGN FEATURES

The design of a tank, which remains true even with the latest MBT (Main Battle Tank) designs of today, revolves around the balance of just three key elements – mobility, firepower and protection. The thicker the armour, the better the protection. The bigger the gun, the bigger the tank needs to be and the heavier it becomes. A bigger, heavier tank, may not fit on bridges or railway wagons, while the weight will put more strain on the engine and transmission and reduce mobility. In simple terms, it is not possible to have all three maximums together; there has to be a balance and some clever designs to get the best. One or two of the German designs at the late stages of the war went beyond what was sensible. The Maus weighed in at over 180 tons (182,888kg). Two prototypes were built,

but what railway or bridge could have coped with that kind of weight? Mobility would have been extremely limited, even though firepower (12.8cm main gun and 7.5cm coaxial) and thick armour would have satisfied the other two requirements.

There was even an intention to build the vast 1,000-ton Landkreuzer P.1000 'Ratte', which would carry two naval 28cm guns in a naval-pattern gun turret. Presented to Hitler in 1943, the design might have gone ahead but was cancelled by armaments minister Albert Speer. No railway could have managed it; it would have been too big to use tunnels, too wide and heavy for bridges; and would still have been a huge target for allied airpower. It is incredible that such a waste of valuable resources could ever have been under consideration.

A modern German tank, a Leopard 1, sectioned at the Defence College, Shrivenham, showing how everything is fitted into an armoured hull.

Detail of the turret and basket of the Leopard 1.

Here is my build of the Takom Ratte, with the two Maus tanks alongside it, built but as yet unpainted.

ARMOURED FIGHTING VEHICLES OTHER THAN TANKS

The fully tracked tank provided an ability to ignore roads and travel cross-country. With more reliable engines and faster speeds, these tanks needed more support, as an infantryman on foot was too slow and vulnerable, so the requirement arose for APCs (Armoured Personnel Carriers). The German army opted for an armoured version of its medium half-track, the SdKfz 251, sometimes simply referred to as the 'Hanomag' after the main manufacturer. Artillery was also needed, so the army began to mount artillery in a tracked chassis to accompany the advancing Panzers. This provided a better cross-country performance than the horse-drawn artillery units supporting the bulk of the German Infantry divisions throughout the war. With the huge developments in air power, there also came a requirement for AA (Anti-Aircraft) defence equipment, which led to the mounting of AA weapons on tank chassis and half-tracks. The half-tracks were fitted with armoured cabs, so as to provide some protection for crews as they accompanied Panzer units in combat areas.

The other main type of AFV was the armoured car, again in a mix of variants. These were used for reconnaissance duties in particular. While there were early four-wheelers that were little more than a car chassis fitted with simple, open-topped armoured bodywork, that was soon replaced with the small SdKfz 221 series of four-wheel drive armoured cars which had a turret on an enclosed armoured body. Also used in the early part of the war was a series of six-wheel (six-rad) armoured cars, later followed by the bigger eight-rad series, which was in service to the end of the war.

As can be seen, there is plenty of scope for the modeller, even without including soft-skin equipment and artillery. However, as we will see later on, combat experience led to interim designs where the vehicle types crossed over to provide an answer to a particular problem.

The PzKpfw II

This light tank was the second of the new Panzers built for the Wehrmacht during the 1930s. It was a bit larger than the Pz I and was armed with a turret-mounted 20mm gun, plus a 7.92mm machine gun coaxially. Experience in the Spanish Civil War had shown the lack of any anti-armour weapon on the Pz I and while the intention was already there to build the Pz III and IV medium tanks, delays meant that a gap needed to be filled. The result was the Pz II.

The Pz II was first produced in 1936 with a series of development machines that tried different road wheel arrangements. These first ones were referred to as the Ausf a (the lower case 'a' differentiates it from a later production variant). With a number of modifications, the Ausf b (again, with a lower case 'b') was built with modified running gear and wider track. The six small road wheels were strengthened by an external beam and there was a rounded transmission cover on the front of the hull. The final version of the development series was the Ausf c (lower case 'c'), with further modifications that were carried into the main production versions, the Ausf A, B and C (the production versions are identified by the use of the capital letters). The production versions saw the use of the five larger road wheels and springs, which became one of the main recognition features of the Pz II. There were various modifications made while these were in service, as over 1,100 were built.

A small number of the later Ausf D were built, with a completely redesigned hull but retaining the same turret. These saw limited service and were withdrawn for conversion to Flammpanzer (flamethrower tanks), or the Ausf D chassis was often used to mount captured Russian 7.62cm anti-tank gun in an armoured superstructure and gun shield. These were referred to as the Marder II, along with others carrying the German 7.5cm Pak 40 using hulls from the main production variants. The Ausf F was the final main production variant, with over 500 being built. The main physical features were: the flat front plate to the hull and the full-width front of the superstructure; a one-piece 30mm flat plate; and a new conical design of the idler wheel. A later version, the Ausf L, commonly referred to as the Luchs (Lynx) was built in 1943–4 for use by reconnaissance units and this had a completely redesigned hull and turret and a new suspension design with interleaved road wheels.

The Pz II chassis was also used for other variants. One of these had a lengthened hull and an extra road wheel and carried the 15cm sIG infantry gun, this time without the full carriage. Just twelve of these were built, with all of them serving in North Africa with the DAK (Deutsches Afrikakorps). Over 600 examples of the Wespe were built, fitting the light field howitzer, the leFH 18 10.5cm. The hull was slightly lengthened and the engine moved forward, leaving space at the back for the open-topped fighting compartment for the gun crew. One other interesting variant to mention is that a small number of armoured bridge layers, or Brükenleger, were built and used by 7th Pz Division in Belgium and France in 1940.

Chapter Three

Tools and Materials – The Basics and Beyond

There is a great variety of tools and materials available to the modeller today and inevitably you will tend to collect more over the years as you continue with your modelling hobby. I will admit to buying particular tools that I have rarely used. At times, they can be just the ticket, but are they essential to basic modelling? In many cases I would suggest not, as there are just a few basic tools that you need in order to get started building models. The others you may buy further down the track as your experience grows, but they can be expensive, while the basic ones are all low cost.

BASIC TOOLS

If you are going to build model armour, let's start at the beginning and think about what sort of basic toolkit you need to have on hand. In terms of plastic models, this will consist of a craft knife, a sprue cutter and glue.

Craft Knife

There are various different craft knives on the market and they all do the same job, so it is really just a question of which one you like using. There

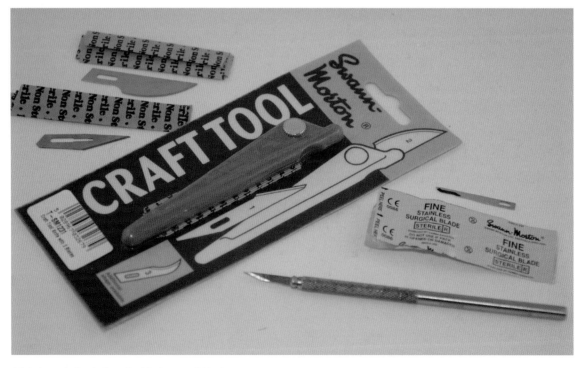

Metal- and plastic-handled knives and blades.

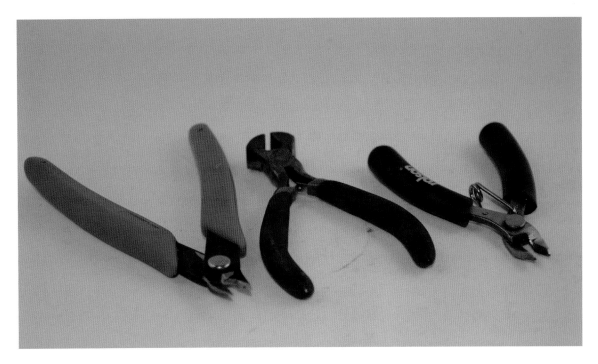

A selection of sprue cutters.

can be small differences in price, though craft knives are not a high-cost item, but essentially it is the size and shape of the handle and what you find comfortable to use. I have spent most of my modelling life using a cheap plastic-handled knife that uses Swann Morton blades in a choice of shapes. Most of the time I have used their curved blade, though sometimes the straight alternative. Over time, a year or two, I find that the top of the handle, either side of the blade, tends to weaken and eventually breaks after a lot of use. However, the shape of the handle is comfortable to hold and use, plus it is cheap to replace.

More recently, I have taken to using a smaller metal knife handle and a straight cutting blade, though other shapes are available. Blades last well and I am finding it comfortable to use. Cutting blades are not expensive, so do replace them when they start to lose their sharp edge. There are other types of knives available, using much larger handles, but personally I don't find these so comfortable. It is a case of trial and error and finding which suits you best.

I must of course add the safety reminder that you should not leave these sharp knives lying around where young children could pick them up, or indeed where other adult members of your household might be unaware of them and could get a nasty cut. It is equally important when using them not to cut towards you and to be very careful of cutting your own fingers. I, like most modellers, have made mistakes and cut my fingers over the years, but I do always take safety seriously and have not had any serious accidents. Though not what I would classify as essential, it is a good idea to invest in a cutting mat. Not only can one save your hands, but also the surface of your table, which for many people will mean a kitchen or dining table, unless you have the luxury of space for a dedicated workbench.

Sprue Cutter

Also referred to as a 'side cutter', I regard this as an essential item, even though scissors can be used if you are stuck. Sprue cutters do not need to be expensive, though better quality ones will last longer. The bottom edge is flat, unlike scissors. There are a couple of options, with either 'straight-cut' or 'cross-cut' cutters. On the 'straight-cut', the blades meet edge-to-edge, while on the 'cross-cut' one blade fits fractionally below the other.

A sprue cutter is used to cut the parts away from the sprue. Any remaining stub on the part can then be cleaned away using a craft knife. I will come back to another good use for the sprue cutter in the preparation of parts during assembly.

Glue

There is a wide variety of glues/adhesives on the market and each one has its pros and cons. The one I use the most is Revell Contacta. Why this one? It is readily available, works well on plastic and has a long, thin metal applicator tube, which allows for good accuracy when applying the glue.

There are too many alternative glues to list here, but there are two others which I use for different jobs. One is Deluxe Materials Plastic Magic, which is a thin liquid cement that comes in a square glass bottle, along with a couple of different size brushes for applying the glue to the plastic mating surface. The other is Extra Thin Plastic Cement from Tamiya, which is again brush-applied. You hold the parts together and apply the cement, which flows into the join by capillary action and gives a nice smooth joint.

If you are going to build resin or metal models, or add etched brass, superglue will be required. Again, there are all sorts of makes on the market,

Revell Contacta glue bottle.

Deluxe Materials Plastic Magic and Tamiya's Extra Thin Cement.

but the main choice is between the thin and thick types and there are circumstances that will suit one over the other. Again, I will come back to this when looking at kit assembly.

Another useful type of glue to have is one for fixing clear parts. There are different makes on the market, though I tend to use Glue 'n' Glaze by Deluxe Materials. Out of the bottle it is white, but dries clear.

EXTRA TOOLS

Following is a list of extra tools that can be very useful if you go on to do a lot of modelling. Some are cheap and readily available, while others are a costly investment. They are listed in no particular order, but all are good to have on hand.

Pin Vice

A pin vice is a small hand-operated drill that can take some very small drill bits. It is inexpensive and you are likely to use it often enough to consider it one of your essential tools. Pin vices can sometimes be bought cheaply in markets; the more expen-

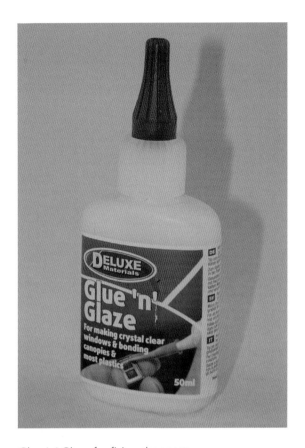

Glue 'n' Glaze for fixing clear parts.

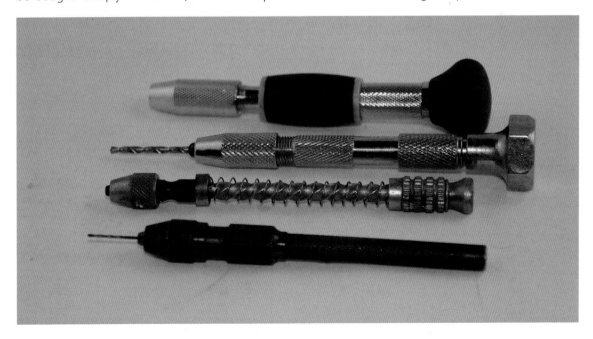

A couple of pin vices, one simple and another with optional chucks.

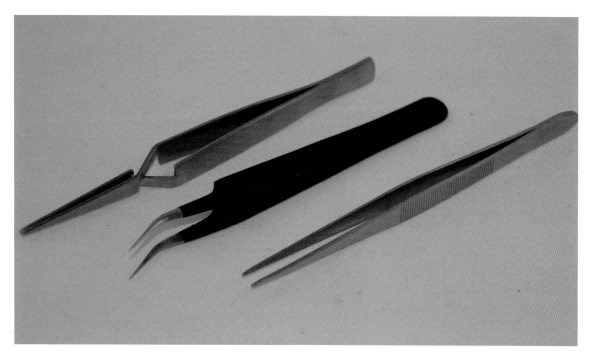

A variety of tweezer styles.

sive ones often include optional 'chucks', the grip which holds the individual drill bits. You can get the drill bits fairly cheaply too, so if they break they are easy enough to replace. For so many jobs, a 1mm drill bit is the most useful, although smaller ones also serve a purpose. You will find that some model kits provide optional parts, which may need a small hole drilling in them. Pin vices are also useful when fitting wire grab handles. I can remember an occasion many years ago when I had used one of the larger type of drills and it was months before I discovered it had another spare chuck hidden inside the handle, giving a total of four different size options in terms of the drill bit it could take.

Tweezers

These are another tool that it is useful to have, ideally several with different-style heads, for example a sharp-pointed pair, an angled head and also one with 'grips' rather than the smoother points. One word of safety regarding the sharp-pointed pair – these can give a painful puncture to fingers if you are not careful. Tweezers are ideal for fitting small

parts in place during a build and also for positioning transfers on your built and painted models. It is best to buy your own, rather than borrow a pair from a female member of the household, who will be less than pleased to find them either missing or returned covered in glue.

Sanding Sticks

The sanding stick is a very useful tool and comes in different grades, just like sandpaper. These are produced by various hobby tool manufacturers (I tend to use the ones from Wilder Productions, which I get through their UK importers, the Airbrush Company). An alternative is to use the ones sold on the high street as nail files, which again are sold in different grades, but these will not work as well as those intended for tougher hobby use.

Needle Files

Similar in some ways to a sanding stick, solid metal needle files are simply more heavy duty. Needle files are smaller than the large DIY types and are designed for use on smaller objects. They come in different shapes to enable them to reach into confined spaces. Helpfully, some are half-round or

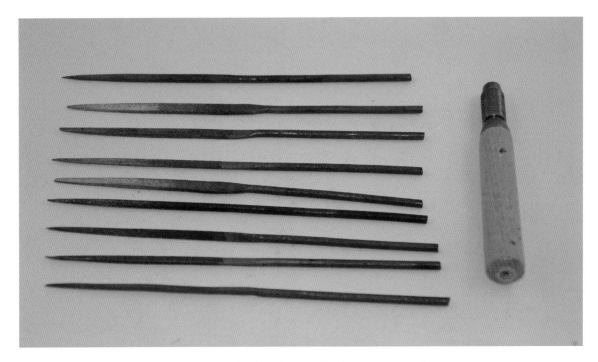

A set of needle files, plus a handle that can be bought to make them easier to grip.

full-round, so are ideal for curves and are useful to have along with flat files for straight edges. These files can be bought inexpensively and the cheaper ones are generally as good as the more expensive alternatives.

There are sets of even smaller ones, known as 'rat-tail files', which are helpful for very fine work. Location holes or the lightening holes in running gear are sometimes in need of cleaning up and these fine files come in really useful.

Hobby Drill

A powered hobby drill is one of the more expensive items in the plastic modeller's toolkit, but one well worth having. As with many things, you can buy some more cheaply than others. I have tried two or three over the years, but my firm favourite is the Dremel brand and I now use the cordless variety.

There are one or two comments to make about them. For drilling small, fine holes I always use a pin vice, but for heavier tasks the powered option is very helpful. It is advisable to invest in a drill with a speed-control facility – if you use

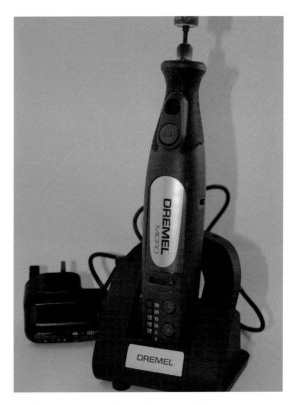

Cordless Dremel drill and charging station.

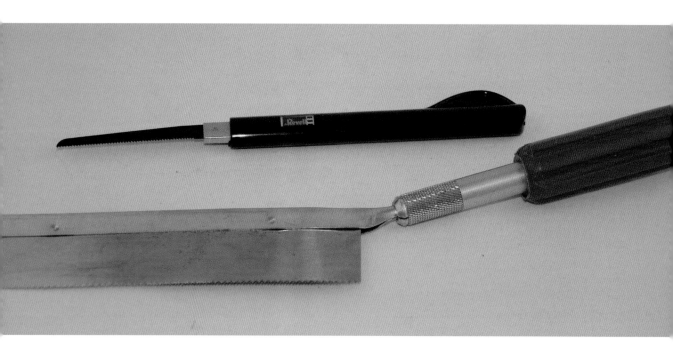

*The common, larger handled saw which is available with different size blades, along
with a small saw in the range of tools available from Revell.*

The finest razor saw I have used is this one from JLC.

too high a speed on the drill, the heat will build up and melt the plastic you are working on. The other big advantage of the powered drill is the variety of different tools that it can use. As well as straightforward drills bits, there are sanding, cutting and polishing discs. If you need to justify the expense, these drills can also come in handy for other household tasks.

Razor Saw

A razor saw is not a tool I use all that often, but I would not be without one. In particular, it is handy for removing large resin casting blocks from resin kit parts. With resin, you can score the line along which you want to remove the block, then snap it off, but with larger, thicker blocks this can easily lead to it an uneven break and the part being damaged, sometimes seriously. Yes, that does mean I've ruined a part more than once over the years in a bid to speed things up. It is much better

to use a razor saw and do the job properly, even if it does take a bit longer. But do bear in mind that a saw actually removes some material and take that into account.

A larger razor saw is the most common, but there are also some smaller bladed options, which are better for finer, more accurate work.

Etched-Brass Folding/Bending Tools

Etched-brass/steel frets with detail parts are common in many kits these days, plus there is a multitude of after-market etched-brass accessory and extra-detailing sets available for many commercial kits. These are common for both AFV models and model aircraft. These folding tools are very helpful indeed and are available in different sizes. I build most of my models in small scale, so the smaller size of folding tool is the one I use most. However, I do still make larger-scale models, so having the bigger option on hand is also helpful. A number of

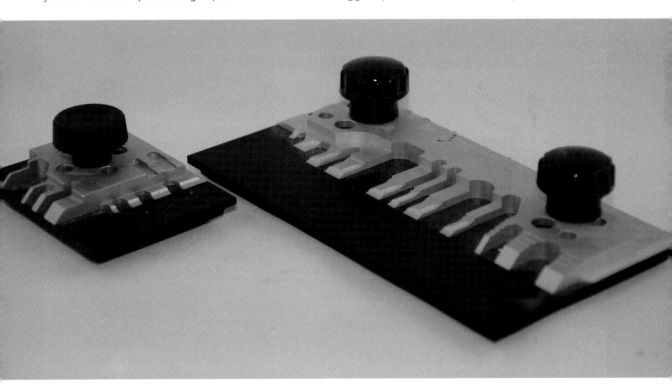

Large and small folding tools, invaluable if you do any work with etched brass.

manufacturers produce these tools; Trumpeter, the plastic kit manufacturer, has started its own range of tools, which includes these at a reasonable price.

Filler/Putty

As with many things, there are plenty of choices on the market for fillers, though I have a couple of favourite ones. Widely available for many years is Green Stuff, but a more recent product is Perfect Plastic Putty from Deluxe Materials. This is very easy to work with and dries quickly without any shrinkage issues. It is a one-part putty, as opposed to a two-part filler, so no mixing is involved. From when it first went on the market a couple of years ago, it quickly became my preferred filler.

Metal Rule

It is very useful to have a metal rule, either a short 6in (15cm) rule or the longer 12in (30cm). The primary use is to help cut clean straight lines on plasticard when using a sharp craft knife. If you want to do some scratch-building or conversions by building your own parts, this is pretty much essential, as with a plastic rule there is the risk of the knife cutting onto the ruler itself and spoiling your neat straight line. A metal rule removes that potential.

OTHER USEFUL MATERIALS

Elastic Bands

The humble elastic band is a very useful tool, in particular for holding larger parts firmly together while glue is drying and preventing the seam opening up before it dries.

Face Masks/Filters

A good-quality face mask is really an essential tool for a number of tasks, particularly when working with polyurethane resin parts. It filters out dust particles and helps to prevent respiratory problems. Prolonged exposure to polyurethane resin dust can lead to a build-up that can result in a cancer. You can use a good-quality paper filter, or, even

Tube of Deluxe Materials' Perfect Plastic Putty.

better, a half-mask fitted with a good-quality filter. I also wear one when using an airbrush. Do not be tempted to get complacent and work without one. The effect of working with these materials can be cumulative, so just get into the habit of wearing a mask or filter at all times when doing so.

Masking Tape

Masking tape is readily available and the rolls come in a variety of thicknesses. For masking straight lines, it is first class. The significant difference to standard 'sticky tape' is that the adhesive is less aggressive, therefore is less likely to damage the paintwork upon removal. That said, this can still happen and remedial work will then be necessary.

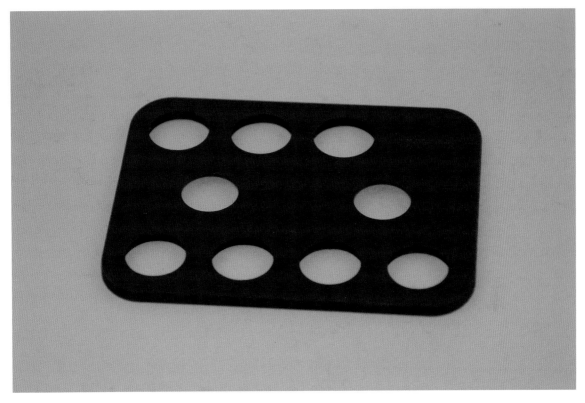

A set of the Quickwheel painting masks, to make painting roadwheels on tanks and half-tracks much easier.

With regard to circular masking, as a modeller of German AFVs you will find that the various road wheels have rubber 'tyres' around them. The range of Quick Wheel masks provides a very useful aid when painting multiple wheels.

Vinyl Gloves

If you work with substances like resins, and metal and also for some painting jobs, it is a good idea to wear gloves. Medical style gloves are available in latex or vinyl. I know some people can have an allergy to latex, so the vinyl ones will be what you need. These are tight-fitting and have the benefit of being very thin, so that you retain the sense of feeling what you are doing without the gloves getting in the way.

Cotton Buds

These are commonly available and not expensive. There are two main styles available, and I make use

of both. My favourite is the one with a pointed bud at one end and a round, flattened end at the other. Both types are available online or in a local chemist, in either the babies section, or more so in the ladies cosmetics section.

Paint Palettes

You can buy paint palettes in any art shop, as well as from online hobby shops. I use a palette all the time when painting, taking paint from the jar on to a palette before applying to a model. I'll talk about this later in the painting section, but you can also make a palette effectively for free by using old plastic bottle tops. Recycle bottle tops rather than throw them away, a win–win solution.

Clamps

For a variety of reasons, plastic kit parts can become slightly warped, so when you glue the parts together, they can try to spring apart. You can try to

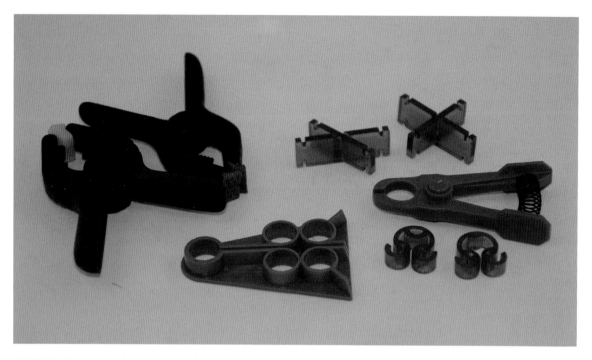

ABOVE: *A variety of clamps.*

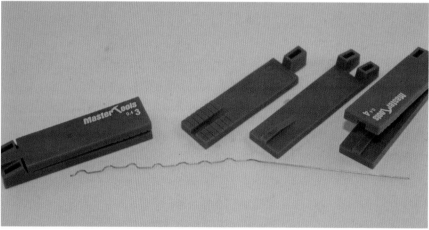

LEFT: *A couple of the grab handle formers and a length of wire with handles ready to be snipped out.*

physically hold them together until the bond takes; the alternative is to use elastic bands or clamps to hold them while the glue sets. Plastic clamps can be bought quite readily and there are some handy ones available in the series of Master Tools by Trumpeter, used together with elastic bands. When you need them, these are really useful.

Grab Handle Former

This is another handy item from Trumpeter's Master Tool range. It is a set of plastic formers that allows you to create wire 'grab handles'. Using thin brass wire, simply press the two halves of the former together to make any number of consistently sized grab handles, ready to be snipped from the length of wire and fitted to your model.

Safety Glasses

If you wear glasses normally, these can do part of the job for you. I have worn glasses most of my life, but there have been a few occasions when odd pieces of resin or plastic have flicked up into my face, no matter how careful I've been. So while they are not essential most of the time, there are some jobs where it can make a real difference. Only recently I was trimming a piece of resin using a craft knife, and a shaving flicked up, went under my glasses and into my eye. I could feel it against my eye and rapidly went to find a mirror to get it out before it caused a problem. A lucky one.

The above is a selection of the tools generally needed for our hobby. There are others, but for projects covered in this book those listed here should cover most circumstances, so let's move on.

THE PZKPFW III

From a 1935 requirement for a tank in the 15-ton class, the first development model, the Ausf A, was produced in small numbers in 1937, with just 15mm of armour. It was armed with a 3.7cm main gun and two coaxial machine guns, with a third in the front of the superstructure. The significant recognition feature was the five large road wheels on each side, although its suspension system needed improvement. The Ausf A was issued to combat units, but was withdrawn to training duties in February 1940.

Only five of the Ausf B were made, and these had eight smaller road wheels on the running gear each side, as did both the Ausf C and D. The Ausf E went into production and this had the torsion-bar suspension on six road wheels each side that was to become standard on all subsequent models. It had improved armour protection and the weight went up to almost 20 tons. All of the Ausf E tanks were built with the 3.7cm main gun, though they were later up-gunned with the 5cm L/42 and a change to an external mantlet.

Further production runs were done for the Ausf F, the Ausf G, H, J, L, M and N, which saw the use of first the longer barrelled 5cm L/60 and then others with the 7.5cm L/24. In 1942, 100 of the Ausf M series were also diverted to be built, armed with a flamethrower in place of the main gun and these did see service on the Eastern Front.

Other variants of the turreted Pz III included a number converted to Tauchpanzer, fitted with wading equipment in readiness for the planned invasion of England, Operation Sea Lion, though they were used in river crossings on the Eastern Front. There were Command (Panzerbefehlswagen) versions using Ausf D, E and H variants, plus further conversions of existing tanks, as well as Artillerie-Panzer Beobachtungswagen (Armoured Observation Post), Bergepanzer III (Armoured Recovery Vehicle) and even an experimental Minenraumpanzer (Mine Destroyer), which featured an extended and raised suspension system, raising the turretless hull much higher off the ground.

The Pz III hull was also the basis for the Sturmgeschütz, an assault gun, which remained in production through to the end of the war. The early versions carried a short 7.5cm StuK37 L/24 and were used in France in 1940, and covered the Ausf A, B and E. Changes in the shape of the superstructure were made and, with the Ausf F, so was the gun to a long-barrelled 7.5cm StuK40 L/43 or L/48. With the Ausf G, production went as high as over 7,500 being built. Another 1,200 were built between 1943–4, mounting the larger 10.5cm StuH42 L/48. The final variant to mention is the Sturm-Infanteriegeschütz 33B, an infantry assault gun. This mounted a 15cm Stu I G L/11 infantry gun in a box-shaped superstructure. Only twenty-four of these were built and they saw service on the Eastern Front.

Chapter Four

Choosing Your Models

I always find which models to choose to be an interesting question, and one we must each answer for ourselves. There is no right or wrong answer – it is all about what you prefer to do in your hobby. Personally, I am interested in history and that a model should represent a specific vehicle from the time and theatre of war in which it was used. I don't have the room for dioramas, so don't build models with these in mind. I also don't build to a particular scale – I like them all. I suppose my first love goes to small scale, 1/76, as this is what was on the market when I started modelling back in the 1960s, thanks to Airfix, Fujimi, Nitto and later Matchbox (now owned by Revell). Only later did ESCI appear with 1/72, now a popular scale for armour models. I also recall when Tamiya first started its 1/35 models. Many of those were motorized, but that was a feature that faded away and their models moved to be static display models, with adults as their main customers more than youngsters. Tamiya's early Schwimwagen and Kübelwagen were among my first purchases, though these have since been superseded by new, more detailed versions.

In recent years I have been making the smaller 15mm scale (about 1/100) models, now that we are seeing more and more being released by the likes of Zvezda and the Plastic Soldier Company. Just to put the scales together in one place for a moment, there are models available in:

- 1/300 and 1/285: used primarily for wargaming
- 1/144 and 1/150: these scales go well with both N-gauge model railways and alongside 1/144 scale aircraft
- 1/100 (15mm scale): used primarily for wargaming

- 1/87: a very popular scale on the Continent, sadly less so here in the UK. Best known are the models by Minitanks, which back in the 1960s also had a tie-in with Airfix here in the UK
- 1/76: very much the starting point for small-scale armour models thanks to the Airfix kits first released in the 1960s. Matchbox, Nitto and Fujimi also adopted this scale
- 1/72 (20mm scale): the Italian-based producer ESCI brought out a large range of AFV models in this scale, as this was the same scale as commonly used for model aircraft. This has now become a popular scale, with models made by Revell and Italeri (who now own the old ESCI moulds)
- 1/56 (28mm scale): a relative newcomer to the market, and again largely driven by the wargames market. Italeri has been working with the popular computer game, 'World of Tanks', releasing models with the game branding. This is a good way to encourage users of the game to get into making physical models as well
- 1/48: various models released over the years from Bandai and Tamiya, who then moved away from the scale until recent years, when Tamiya introduced a growing range of excellent models that can also accompany the popular aircraft models in the same scale
- 1/32: a scale which has been used for a few models, such as the old Airfix Rommel's Half-Track, an SdKfz 250 Command vehicle. I recall Monograms also did some, such as the StuG IV and the Wirbelwind
- 1/35: this scale was made popular by Tamiya and Italeri. It has been the huge growth area since the 1970s, with new manufacturers like Trumpeter,

A selection of SdKfz 232 8-rad armoured cars, in 1/100, 1/72, 1/48 and 1/35.

Dragon, Meng, Takom, HobbyBoss, IBG, ICM and others, with lots of resin models and conversions in the same scale
- 1/16 (120mm scale): kits in this scale are relatively new, but Trumpeter now does things like the Tiger I and Tiger II, Panzer IV and suchlike. The downside of these is, however much detail they have and the price, how many can you keep at home once you have built them?
- 1/6: outside the scope of this book, but if you have several thousand pounds available for each model, metal models with remote-control systems, audio effects for gunfire and engine noise are a popular scale. You can often see this scale displayed at events such as Tankfest, Duxford and War and Peace, to name just a few. Very impressive, but equally very expensive.

As you can see from the above, it is worth taking a little time to consider what scale(s) you want to work in.

TYPES (WHEELED, HALF-TRACK, FULL-TRACK)

Do you have a particular interest? There can be all sorts of themes to a collection. You might have favourites and one example I recall was once a bit of a problem, but these days is easy enough to obtain. This is a set of the different Panzers used during the war, with Panzers I, II, III, IV, V (Panther) and VI (Tiger). When I started modelling, it was only possible to get the Airfix Tiger and Panther and the StuG III. I can remember my excitement when Fujimi first released its Pz I Ausf B and later ESCI produced not only the Pz I, Pz II and Pz III, but with different variants as well. There are wheeled armoured vehicles (armoured cars, some trucks), half-tracks, self-propelled artillery, tank destroyers and the Panzers themselves.

Over the years I have found my core interests remain, but have expanded into other areas as well. Some trucks, particularly those fitted with

AA guns, were given armoured cabs to provide a little protection for their crews and also armoured cars such as the early Kfz 13, the lighter four-wheel series and the heavier six- (six-rad) and eight-wheel (eight-rad) machines. I still find it interesting that while the Allies did not adopt eight-wheelers during the war, their influence continues to this day with the Fuchs used by the Bundewehr and the Warsaw Pact's BTR-60, -70 and -80 series, while the US Army (among others) is now a large-scale user of the Stryker.

Then there are the half-track machines and here you have armoured examples, such as the light SdKfz 250 and the medium SdKfz 251 series. The variations on these can easily make up a collection all by themselves.

There are also armoured cabs fitted to otherwise unarmoured variants, again particularly for mobile Flak guns plus some specialist armoured vehicles, such as the armoured Command version of the SdKfz 7 used by the V2 units late in the war. There are lots of options in these.

As for the Panzers, they vary from the small Pz I through to the King Tiger and even the Maus, a 160-ton tank being developed at the end of the war, though only two were built. Over the last couple of years there has also been a growth in fascination for the so-called 'Paper Panzers', the designs that were only on the drawing board when the war ended.

If you can manage the expense, these huge 1/16 models complete with radio control are impressive. Seen on the stand of Armortek at Tankfest.

SCALES

As we have seen above, there are a number of scales to choose from for your models. You can go from the small wargaming scales of 1/300 and 1/285 through to the recent addition of 1/16. You may also see references to scales in another format, most often in relation to wargames, such as: 15mm, which equals 1/100; 20mm, which equals 1/76 or 1/72; 28mm, which equals 1/56; and 120mm, which equals 1/16. Which you choose is a question of personal choice about levels of detail, the cost of kits, the space you have to store them and so on.

MATERIAL

The most common material used for models is the injection-moulded plastic kit. However, there are also models available made in either polyurethane resin or white metal. These last two are especially used by the smaller model producers and are made in relatively small numbers compared to the large plastic kits. I have sometimes heard a modeller say they 'don't build resin/metal models'. However, if you are after a particular subject, this could be the only source of the model that you want to add to your collection, so my advice would be to just have a go. These models may use different glues from plastic, but essentially there is little difference and I will tackle what's involved in the next chapter.

COMPLEXITY

Complexity is another significant element to consider. This is again very personal and can of course change during your lifetime in the modelling hobby. If something is too complex for a beginner, they may find they don't get a result quickly enough, so become frustrated and give up. I remember being given the Airfix Churchill kit when I was very young and found the small wheels and suspension units very fiddly. That nearly put me off tank kits for life, but then an aunt bought me the old Airfix Sherman and I discovered that not all tanks were the same and I haven't looked back since. However, as a modeller approaches more advanced years, eyesight and dexterity may not be as good as they once were, so in that case it might be convenient to return to building the smaller, more straightforward kits.

The quest for 'more detail' seems to be a constant pressure on manufacturers, and technology has been a significant enabling factor. We can take it down to a parts count for a kit and in many 1/35 scale models these days we are regu-

larly seeing this count exceeding 1,000 parts, and if you add additional etched-brass details it can go much higher. Some of the parts can be very small and removing them from their sprues, then cleaning up the attachment points, can be a time-consuming and sometimes tedious task. I am sure some will disagree with me, but I hear a number of modellers say they get bored with a model they are building and it is consigned to the shelf while they start on something else that may give a quicker result. These kits with a high parts count will also mean a much higher price bracket. It is not unusual to see prices around the £100 mark or more these days, another indication that they are aimed more at an adult customer and are not 'pocket-money' toys.

There are models available that which have either part or full interior details for turrets, fighting compartments and engine compartments. These are more involved and do obviously take longer to build, with the build and painting sequence needing to be planned in advance. What this does help with, though, is understanding more about the structure of a tank, where the weak points

More of the large 1/16 radio control models, nicely finished.

are/were and how everything fits into the confines of an armoured box. At the Tank Museum at Bovington, there is a Centurion that has been cut right down the middle, so you can see just how tightly everything fits inside, including the crew, of course.

One particular feature of many modern armour kits that creates mixed reactions in how the manufacturer goes about making the tracks. The older kits use a single-piece soft vinyl style one-piece option, sometimes referred to as the 'rubber-band' style. These don't make it easy to create the effects of track sag, caused by the weight of the metal track links and how tightly the track is fitted around the running gear. One solution is to have individual link tracks that need to be assembled link by link. The drawback of these is the time taken to remove all the parts from the sprues and clean up the moulding feed points from each link. If, as in some cases, there is more than one part per link, this can be a very time-consuming process, which can put some people off. Dragon Models have tried to address this by including what they call 'Magic Tracks', where the links are supplied in poly bags, usually two bags, one for each track, saving the modeller from the tedium of removing them from the sprues. Another alternative is the so-called 'link and length' style, where the straight sections of track are moulded as one piece, with individual links to build up around the drive sprockets and idlers, and sections of the top run of track moulded with pre-shaped 'sag'. You then join these sections together to the style and length required by your model. The third variation is another Dragon Models development, and that is the inclusion of very well detailed one-piece tracks moulded in what they have called 'Dragon Styrene', or DS track. This is easy to use and the two ends can be simply glued together. It has very cleanly moulded detail and can be painted without any problems.

An aftermarket option which many modellers like is to replace whatever track is supplied in the kit with the metal-cast individual track links from Fruil Model. These are beautifully made, add a bit of weight to your model and give all the natural sag you might want. However, they take some time to assemble and, being metal, will need a coat of primer before painting, plus they do add another cost to your model. As with most things, there is no right or wrong about which method to choose – it's down to personal preference.

Another aspect to complexity, particularly for smaller scale models, is that wargamers tend to want to build a number of models for a unit, get them finished quickly, paint them and get them into action on a gaming table. But it is important not to fall into the trap of differentiating between modellers and wargamers – if you attend any of the wargame shows you will see some stunning modelling on display, even though many of those attending would describe themselves as wargamers rather than modellers. The result of this has been evident in recent years, with the growth in production of plastic kits, not just resin models, where the running gear and tracks of a tank are moulded in one piece, or maybe just a few more as perhaps the outer discs of the drive sprocket and idler are separate parts. Even the larger manufacturers such as Dragon, Italeri and Zvezda have moved down this path in the last few years. Others, such as S-Model, the Plastic Soldier Company and Armourfast, have made growing businesses using this format. The other thing about these is that they often feature multiple models in the box, which is ideal for wargames units.

In sum, if you like complexity and detail, there are many kits on the market for you, but if prefer something simpler, plenty of these are also available. Personally, I happily mix and match according to the subject matter which appeals to me. Of course, your budget and access to the models you want will also be a consideration. And as noted earlier, for the older modeller eyesight and dexterity can become a problem, making the task of building a kit more difficult. A solution for many might be to collect the increasing number of ready built and painted models that are now being marketed by Dragon, Zvezda, Modelcollect, Oxford Diecast and others.

Looking not too dissimilar to the Pz III, the Pz IV was developed in the mid-1930s as a tank in the 20-ton class. The suspension consisted of four pairs of leaf spring-mounted wheels, so eight road wheels on either side, and four return rollers in addition to the front drive sprocket and rear idler. From the outset, it was fitted with the 7.5cm KwK L/24. The first three versions, Ausf A, B and C, were only built in small numbers; it was the Ausf D which had the first significant production run, with 229 of the gun tanks produced between 1939–41. A particular recognition feature of these early variants was the stepped front plate on the hull. With a number of relatively minor modifications, the Ausf E was also built in similar numbers.

More changes were made with the Ausf F, with thicker armour and the front plate of the hull superstructure changed to a straight flat plate, among other detail changes. It was with the Ausf F that another significant change was introduced, as the F1 had the short 7.5cm KwK 37 L/24 whereas the F2 had the much longer gun barrel of the 7.5cm KwK40 L/43. When these longer barrelled Pz IVs were used in North Africa, they were often referred to as 'Mk IV Specials' thanks to the more capable main gun. The Ausf G was pretty much the same as the F2 with only detail changes, though nearly 1,700 of them were manufactured. Then came the Ausf H, with frontal armour thickness increased from 50mm to 80mm and internally it used a new transmission. Among other modifications that were introduced was the deletion of the side vision ports for the driver and radio operator, plus the use of all-steel return rollers and an AA machine-gun mounting for the commander's cupola. These also frequently were fitted with extra Schürzen side armour on both hull and turret. Over 3,700 of the Ausf H were built between 1943–4. The final variant was the Ausf J, which had a few more changes, including the change to only three return rollers. Internally, the electric traverse and associated auxiliary engine were removed and the space used for extra fuel. The other visual recognition point was the change in the exhaust arrangement, with two vertical exhausts on the rear of the hull. Over 1,700 of the Ausf J were built between mid-1944 and March 1945. The Pz IV was the only German tank to remain in production throughout the war.

As a successful design, it is little wonder that the Pz IV chassis was used for a wide variety of special purpose AFVs. Like the Pz III, a few were converted to Tauchpanzer, submersible tanks for use in Operation *Sea Lion*, though they also went on to serve on the Eastern Front. A Command/Observation variant was the Panzer Beobachtungswagen. The Sturmpanzer IV (Assault Infantry Gun) the Brummbär, had a tall, fixed superstructure and mounted a 15cm StuH43 L/12. A Sturmgeschütz IV involved the fitting of the superstructure used on the StuG III fitted to a Pz IV chassis, plus an extended armoured cover for the driver. Over 1,000 were built from the end of 1943 to the end of the war in March 1945.

Three variations of the Jagdpanzer IV were produced as tank hunters, one with the 7.5cm Pak39 L/48 and the other two with the 7.5cm PaK 42 L/70. Another tank hunter on the Pz IV chassis was the Hornisse/Nashorn, which had the engine moved forward and then an open-top, lightly armoured superstructure for the gun crew and mounting the powerful 8.8cm PaK 43/1 L/71 gun. Nearly 500 of these were built between early 1943 and the end of the war in 1945, and they saw action in Italy as well as on the Eastern Front and in North-West Europe. Then with bodywork very similar to the Nashorn, the Hummel ('Bumble-bee') carried the 15cm sFH18/1 L/30, which was organized in batteries of six and also with ammunition carriers that were the same basic vehicle, but with the gun aperture plated over. Another interesting design for an SP artillery piece was the 10.5cm Heuschrecke ('Grasshopper') which carried the gun in a removable turret along with a gantry, so that it could be removed and emplaced or towed on a wheeled platform.

A number of different self-propelled (SP) anti-aircraft (AA) mounts used the Pz IV chassis, including the Möbelwagen (Removal Van) carrying either a single 3.7cm FlaK 43 L/60, or the four-barrelled 2cm Flakvierling which had simple flat, folding sides. The same weapons were used in the armoured turrets of the Wirbelwind ('Whirlwind') with the Flakvierling and the Ostwind ('East Wind') having the single 3.7cm FlaK.

At the end of the war a twin 3cm MK103/38 was ordered, the Kugelblitz, though only two were completed before the war ended. About twenty Brückenleger ('Bridge Layer') were built and used by Panzer Divisions in 1940. The chassis was also used for the ammunition carrier for the huge rounds of the Karl mortar, as the Munitionschlepper for Karlgerat. Other variants built in small numbers included a turretless recovery Bergepanzer IV and a couple of Assault Bridges that carried a 50m extending fire-fighting ladder for use as an assault bridge for infantry assault. Finally, as models of them are available from Dragon, the suspension was used on the two prototypes of the Panzerfahre, a tracked amphibious armoured ferry.

Chapter Five

Out of the Box – Building Basic Models

In this chapter, I will go through the basics of building models using the most popular materials of injection-moulded plastic, polyurethane resin and white metal. I will build them in what is described as 'OOB', or Out Of the Box, that is, built without any modifications. This is in order to illustrate the basic building techniques that apply to each style of model. After that, I will look at the wide variety of models in the various scales that are available on the market.

One of the most essential elements is building the kit correctly in the first place. While I have learnt this the hard way, by making mistakes over the years, I still see other experienced modellers sometimes writing about how parts of a kit do not fit correctly, yet I know that when building the same kit I did not experience any problems. Something must therefore have gone wrong for them. Hence I will be concentrating on the basic techniques, rather than focusing on the actual kit.

SMALL-SCALE MODELS

Plastic Kit – S-Model 1/72 Kfz 13

For our first model, I will use an example of a 1/72 plastic kit featuring the small Kfz 13 Maschinengewehrkraftwagen, a light armoured car equipped with only with a single MG34, used by the Wehrmacht in the 1930s and into the early stages of World War II before it was retired as obsolete. It is a double kit by S-Model and is available through the Plastic Soldier Company, who import them to the UK, so you get two complete models

in the box. My intention with this is simply to go through the process for building any plastic kit.

So, let's start by opening the box, taking the parts out of the bag and checking both the kit parts and the instructions. This particular kit is quite simple, but a basic rule is to go through the instructions, to see if there are any build options, and to check the colours and marking schemes that are provided for with transfers (decals) in the kit. This may seem a really basic step, but in many kits, especially the larger scale ones, there will be various options for parts and positioning them (such as open or closed hatches as just one example). In some kits it may also mean drilling open specific location holes for optional parts, depending on which kit option you are building. These need to be done before certain elements are joined together, so it is an important thing to check for. I am the first one to admit that there have been times over the years when I have rushed into an assembly and missed this step, thereby learning the lesson the hard way.

Once you have made your decisions, turn to the first stage in the instructions and begin the build. Start by following the construction sequence provided by the manufacturer. Check the parts you need for stage 1 and remove these from the sprue. Use a side cutter to remove them, then clean up those points with a sharp craft knife. Please bear in mind that these blades are like razors, so always use them with care and never leave them lying around, especially if there are young children in the house. You may find that different manufacturers arrange the attachment points in different ways. The parts may have a 'stepped', or possibly

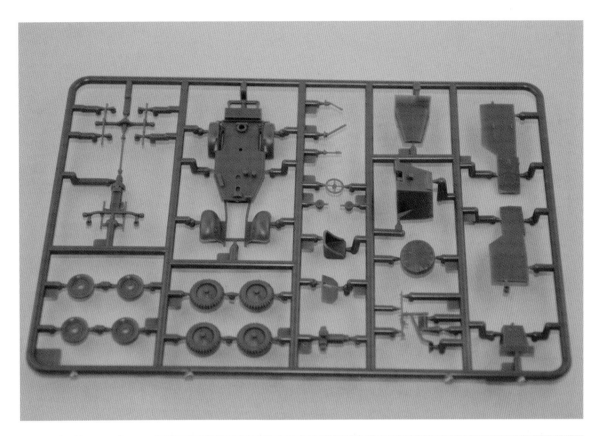

ABOVE: *The kit parts for the S-Model Kfz 13 on the sprue, which is the name for the frame on which all the parts are moulded.*

RIGHT: *The drive train and floor pan done and joined, bodywork ready to be fitted.*

The assembled but unpainted model.

chamfered, edge to key the fit against an adjacent part. Do be careful how you clean up the cut attachment point. On the stepped edges, if they are not cleaned up correctly this will interfere with the fit of the parts during assembly. That brings us to the next important step, which is to test the fit by holding the parts together, usually referred to as 'dry fitting', so as to ensure that everything is fitting together correctly before you commit to applying the glue. This is one of the key elements to getting the assembly right.

In the case of the Kfz 13, the first stage is to assemble the lower frame of the springs, axles and wheels. With that done, leave it on one side for the glue to set. To move on, identify the parts you need for stage 2, which in this case are the body floor along with internal details of the driver's seat, gear and handbrake levers, plus the pintle-mounted machine gun. The headlights also need to be fitted onto the front wings. Let these set. You might choose to paint these interior parts at this stage, although with such an open-top vehicle as this, I would choose not to do so yet. Stage 3 is to fit stages 1 and 2 together.

For stage 4, again identify the parts from the sprue, remove them, clean them up and dry-fit to check how everything fits together. Add the steering wheel, the shield to the MG, the rear armour panel, plus the spare wheel.

The last part of the build stage is to assemble the main armour bodywork, the radiator cover, bonnet and side armour panels. With them together, fit the bodywork to the floorpan/chassis. With this particular kit, there is also a small fret of etched-metal details, for the rear number plate, width indicators, rear-view mirror and pennant holder, plus a hand bar across the open top of the crew compartment. To fix etched parts to plastic, you will need to use superglue.

The etched parts come on a metal fret, which is a carrier frame essentially the same as the sprue for plastic parts. To remove the parts from the fret,

it helps to have a hard cutting plate, such as a piece of Perspex. Then use a sharp craft knife to cut the parts from the fret. Use a metal rule to help keep the cut as exact as possible to the edge of the part. Another tip is to use a piece of clear tape to ensure that the released part doesn't 'ping off' the fret to be lost to the dreaded carpet monster, or worse, up into your eye. It is a good idea to wear safety glasses when you do this, if the parts are not held securely.

That is the end of the assembly and includes the very basic lessons for assembling a plastic kit of any scale or subject. We will move on to painting and markings in the next chapter.

Metal Model – MMS StuG III Ausf A
I considered various models for this section, such as a Panzer II Ausf A or the unusual little Borgward BIV

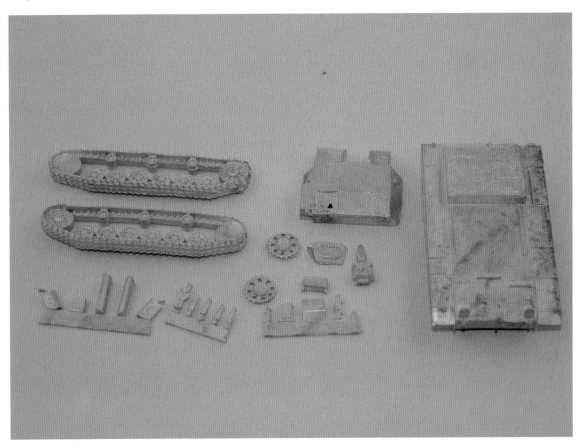

The kit parts for the MMS Stug III Ausf A laid out.

Ausf C Demolition Vehicle. In the end, due to the widespread popularity of the subject, I decided on an early variant of the StuG III. Start by laying out the parts in the pack.

Next, give all the parts a wash in a mild detergent (such as washing-up liquid in water) and let them dry thoroughly. The reason for doing this is due to the way in which metal models are moulded. They are cast with molten metal in a centrifugal casting machine, using a vulcanized rubber mould. A light dusting of powder (essentially talcum powder) is put inside the rubber moulds as a release agent to assist in getting the castings out and avoiding damage to the production mould. Any remnants of that powder can have an effect on either glues or paint, hence the wash to make sure it's all gone.

There is a small page of assembly instructions, with an exploded assembly diagram that indicates where all the parts are to be fitted. Having studies that, the first step is to look at the two main hull parts. These are the one-piece lower hull plus the superstructure of the fighting compartment.

The superstructure has the option to fit one set of hatches open; the ones on the other side are moulded shut. If you want to leave the one hatch open to enable you to add a crew figure (not included in the kit but available separately), you need to open up the thin metal flash in the opening. This can be done easily with a sharp craft knife and the edges finished off with a needle file. Then, on the back of the superstructure, there are some casting marks from the metal feed points

The MMS metal model assembled and waiting to be given a coat of primer.

Assembled model of the StuG III Ausf A.

to be cleaned away, along with a little metal flash. ('Flash' is a term for excess material, which, under the pressure of casting, seeps into any gap between the two halves of the mould. This also happens on plastic kits.)

Do a similar check on the main hull and clean away any marks from the casting feeds, which in this case are on the front of the glacis plate and a little on the edge of the right-side track guard. Then there are a couple of holes in the rear track guards, one round and one oblong, which need to be opened up. These allow for the lights to remain visible in the event the rear sections are folded up and would otherwise stop the light from being seen. In addition to this, there are various locating holes which need to be drilled out, for fitting the notek light, the vehicle jack and the fire extin-

guisher. I always use the manual pin vice to do this, fitted with a 0.8mm drill bit in this instance.

Check the fit of the outer ring of the drive sprocket, which is moulded with the track teeth only on the section between the upper and lower track run; the other parts are as if they are 'hidden' within the tracks themselves. Clean up any remnants of the casting feeds, which can still be done with a basic craft knife. Dry-fit the parts again, just as you would with a plastic kit, before fitting the track units in place with superglue. Any type works, though I personally prefer a gel type as this also helps as a gap filler. Then add the two shock absorbers each side, where indicated on the exploded assembly diagram, but these need to be trimmed to fit. So add the track units first and keep dry-fitting the shock absorbers and trimming

Assembled and primed model of the StuG III Ausf A.

the base of the part until it fits correctly. Use a pair of tweezers to put them in place – you may need to do this several times until the fit is right. There is a little diagram on the instruction sheet that shows how they should look. Finally, fix them in place with superglue.

With metal models, solder can be used for assembly, but as these are cast in a low-melt metal alloy, there is a significant danger of melting the smaller parts, hence I suggest using the superglue. Again, leave this assembly on one side for the glue to set properly. Twenty-four hours is about right before moving on to adding all the detail fittings.

If you have not already done so, identify all the fittings and where they need to be placed. Remove them from their carrier strip, which is the casting feed as well. This can be done by scoring the join between the strip and the part; then bend the part and it will snap off. For really small, fine parts, cut them off completely rather than trying to snap them off. An alternative method is to use side cutters to snip off the carrier as with these MMS kits it is quite thin. This particular kit does not have a lot of parts – just the air intakes, exhausts, toolbox, notek light, fire extinguisher, jack and jack block, hatch (which is simple to split in two if you want it open), gun mounting and the smoke grenade box. Using superglue, these are all easy enough to fit and the build itself is complete. Assembling the parts is pretty much the same as any plastic kit, so don't let the idea of a metal model put you off.

Resin Model – Milicast 1/76 SdKfz 251/17 Ausf C (2cm Flak) (Luftwaffe Version)

As with any kit, start by opening the pack and checking/identifying all the parts. Like metal kits, resin models are usually moulded with the use of a powdered release agent to help extend the usable life of the moulds, so the parts need to be washed in a mild detergent and left to air-dry. With resin models, there is the potential for parts to become warped after they come out of the mould. If that is the case, put them (carefully) in very hot water and, when the resin becomes flexible, bend the piece back to shape, then put it under the cold tap to fix the revised shape. Again, leave it to dry.

Resin models can also have blemishes on parts due to air bubbles getting in to the resin when it was mixed or put into the mould. However, most manufacturers of resin parts use a vacuum chamber these days for mixing the resin and then moulding the parts. This takes the likelihood of air bubbles to a minimum, so they are much rarer nowadays. If there is an obvious air bubble, just fill it with something like Green Stuff or my favourite, Deluxe Materials' Perfect Plastic Putty. If a part is unformed, so the bubble means a piece of the part is simply not there, contact the supplier who will usually be happy to provide a replacement for you. Fortunately, there were no such air bubble blemishes to deal with in this Milicast model.

This is one of the most visually interesting variants of the 251 series, as it has extended sides that could be folded down to allow for the fitting of a 2cm Flak 38 within the body, while also creating

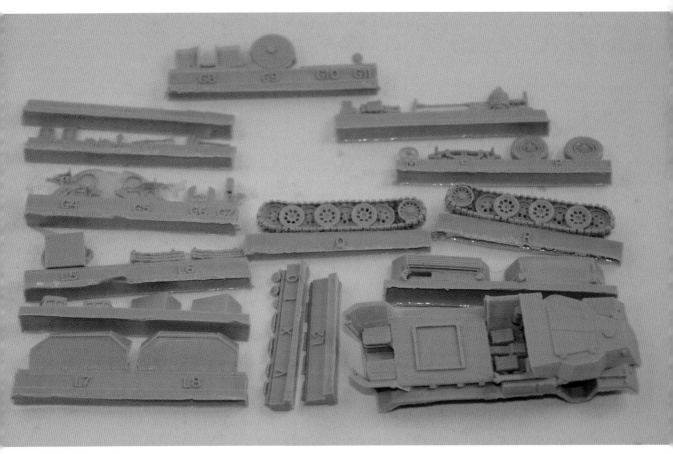

Kit parts for the SdKfz 251/17 laid out.

The primed half-track and gun.

the extra space to allow it to have a 360-degree traverse, with the full gun shield retained, plus space for the gun crew to serve the weapon.

Milicast not only provides a parts list against which you can check the kit, but also clearly identifies the individual parts using numbers or letter on the casting feed block that carries the smaller detail fittings.

There may also be some flash, consisting of a web of thin resin that has seeped between the two parts of the mould. Remove it with a sharp craft knife. In this model, you will find some in the two sides of the gun mount, rings in which

the gun itself is mounted. The resin gun barrel needs to be carefully removed from the casting feed. If you want to make a slight improvement, you could replace the barrel with a turned metal replacement, though in my case I've kept it with the part supplied in the kit.

The same basic construction sequence is to identify the parts needed for each step of the build, prepare them, then build the model. Dry-fit the parts before applying any superglue. Bear in mind that with superglue you only get a limited time to adjust the position of the parts, so it is even more important to check by dry-fitting first.

With the two elements of the model built, the half-track itself and the 2cm Flak are ready to be given a coat of primer. Once that is dry, it will be ready for painting.

Another Plastic Kit – Jagdpanzer E100

Let's turn back to another plastic kit for a moment. A popular subject these days, in both large and small scales, are the so-called 'Paper Panzers', the designs that the German companies were working on towards the end of the war. One of these was the E100, and as well as the basic gun tank there was to be a Jagdpanzer variant, armed with a large 128mm gun, that makes me think of it as a 'Jagdpanther on steroids'.

The kit to look at now is from Modelcollect, a Chinese-based company that is one of the relative newcomers to our list of manufacturers, but which has quickly built up a large and varied range of models.

The build of the basic kit is quite straightforward, following the techniques already described. The three particular things about this one are the inclusion of a turned-brass barrel, some etched-brass details and metal springs that provide a working suspension.

The use of a turned-metal gun barrel rather than a plastic one in two halves means that there is no joint seam. There is also a perforated muzzle brake, which uses another etched-metal part that wraps around the muzzle. In order to get that part to wrap around the end of the barrel, the etched-metal parts have some inherent 'spring' in them. To eradicate this, it is best to anneal the etched part(s) first, by heating it in a candle flame, or maybe the flame on a gas hob. Clearly this needs to be done with great care. For younger modellers, do it only with the help/supervision of an adult. Do not hold the parts in your fingers – the metal will transmit the heat and you will burn yourself. Use a holder, such as a wooden (not plastic) clothes peg. The metal will tend to discolour but only needs to be in the flame for a few seconds, just so that the metal heats up. Then put it into cold water so you that don't burn your fingers by touching the metal. This heating process removes that 'spring' and you will find the part bends neatly around the barrel.

The suspension on this model is a little fiddly to assemble. It uses small metal springs that fit to the suspension arms when these are fitted to the hull. Fix each end of the metal springs on to the locating lugs with a touch of superglue; if you get this right, you will have a working suspension on your model. If you find it awkward, an alternative is just to glue everything to fix it in place.

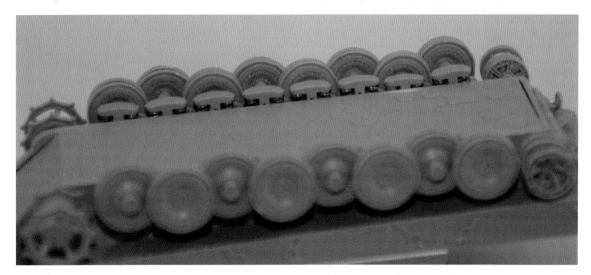

The working suspension of the Modelcollect kit.

LEFT: *The built and unpainted model in progress, still without the track guards, but with the unpainted track temporarily fitted. You can see the brass gun barrel and the simple engine detail before the decking is fitted.*

BELOW: *The model with a coat of primer.*

Here is the next stage, with basic coat of Dunkelgelb, the tracks painted in a base colour and the track guards fitted.

Build the hull and running gear, but at this stage don't fit the large track guards. Add the other etched-brass detail fittings, such as the mesh grills on the engine deck.

The track and running gear need basic painting and the track fitting before the track guards are added. So the next thing to do, as there are both plastic and brass parts, is to give the whole model a coat of grey primer before adding a base coat of Dunkelgelb (German World War II Europe tan colour). This gets the model itself built and the basic groundwork done for the painting and weathering, which we will finish off in the next chapter.

LARGE-SCALE MODELS
Armoured Krupp Protze
Kfz 69 with 3.7cm Pak 36

Building a tank in the larger scale of 1/35 is quite straightforward, so in considering what to build as an example I decided to go for something a bit more unusual than the commonly seen Tiger or Panther. I selected a recent kit from Bronco Models, an armoured truck and 3.7cm anti-tank gun. This was not a mainstream production variant, but a stop-gap design as a result of combat experience early in World War II. The German tanks were accompanied by towed anti-tank guns, a tactic used throughout the war. In the early stages, they used a soft-skin truck, the Krupp Kfz 69 with a towed 3.7cm Pak 36. In the front line, the unarmoured truck and the towed gun left the crew exposed, especially as there was a delay in getting the gun unhitched and set up in a firing position. The same delay occurred when getting the gun out of action to move on. The answer was to fit simple armoured panels over the front of the truck and take the gun off the usual carriage and fit it to the rear deck of the truck, adding an enlarged shield as well.

As is common with Bronco Models, there is a lot of very fine detail in the model and etched parts are included as well to add even finer details. So it can look a bit daunting as a build, but it is such an interesting subject. What we will do is to go through the build following the sequence of the kit instruction booklet and let the photos tell the build story. It is not actually difficult when you just take it step by step.

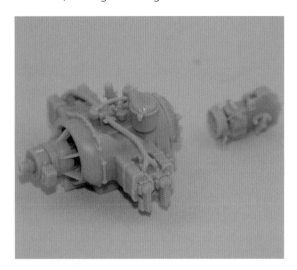

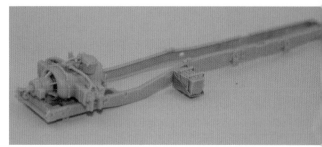

LEFT: *The first stage in the build is to assemble the engine. This does include some tiny parts for butterfly nuts. Be very careful when removing these from the sprue as they can easily get lost. (If you find they are too small for you, because this area is hidden from view it is not a problem to leave them off.)*

ABOVE: *This shows how the engine fits neatly to the chassis, which also has an etched part for the battery tray.*

LEFT: *Next add the engine firewall. This needs the steering column to be inserted through a small hole, which has a bracket on it that needs a little bit of 'forcing' to get it through as the hole is quite small.*

Now we have the engine, firewall, battery box, fuel tank and drive train all fitted to the chassis.

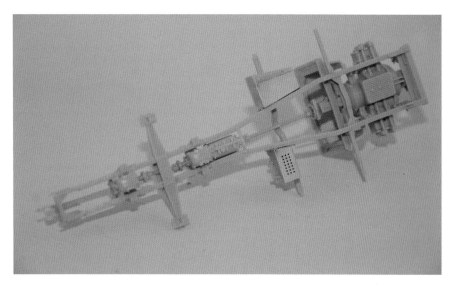

The rear suspension is fitted and the wheels prepared to be fitted The wheel hubs were sprayed with Panzer Grey before fitting the rubber tyres that come with the kit. This is easier than painting them with the tyres in place. These will be left on one side and not fitted until the build is complete.

Now the driver's footwell is built and ready for fitting to the chassis, with gear lever, handbrake and foot pedals in place while they are easy to reach to get the parts in place. Note the etched pads on the foot pedals for extra detail.

This shows a separate subassembly, the 3.7cm Pak 36, with a larger shield and ready-use ammunition boxes in etched trays fitted to the inside of the gunshield.

With front and rear mudguards added, along with the bonnet, I chose to give the whole thing a spray with Panzer Grey at this stage, as some elements here will be difficult to get at once other parts are in place and any light grey plastic would be very noticeable later on.

With the rear body and gun fitted, the seats are painted with a red leather colour, and given a brown wash which is then largely removed with a damp cotton bud to leave a worn leather effect.

At the back, two crew seats and rear foot steps are added. These rear parts are relatively fragile, so I left them off until the final stages – here you see them fitted. The kneeling pads for the gun crew are painted with the leather effects as well.

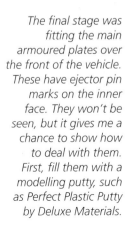

The final stage was fitting the main armoured plates over the front of the vehicle. These have ejector pin marks on the inner face. They won't be seen, but it gives me a chance to show how to deal with them. First, fill them with a modelling putty, such as Perfect Plastic Putty by Deluxe Materials.

Let it dry, then sand flat with a sanding stick. It is now ready for painting before fitting on to the truck.

The completed model, before adding transfers and weathering.

Wheeled Vehicle (AFV Club SdKfz 232)

I have already covered the basics of building a plastic kit and the techniques apply to any one of them. In larger scale models, there is generally a chance to include much more detail in the kit, both inside and out. Just to take one example, let's have a look at the AFV Club kit of the SdKfz 232, one of the variants of the eight-rad series of armoured cars. This one has an open-top fighting compartment and carries a 7.5cm infantry support gun.

AFV Club SdKfz 232, front three-quarters view. AFV CLUB

AFV Club SdKfz 232, rear three-quarters view. AFV CLUB

AFV Club SdKfz 232, fighting compartment detail, view 1. AFV CLUB

AFV Club SdKfz 232, fighting compartment detail, view 2. AFV CLUB

Half-Track (Tamiya SdKfz 251/1 Ausf C)

It is many years ago that Tamiya released its kit of the SdKfz 251 Ausf C half-track, complete with some crew figures. The style of the kit is showing its age these days and the quality of the figures is not as good as more modern productions, but as a basic kit it is still good. It is still on sale and at a very competitive price for a 1/35 scale kit.

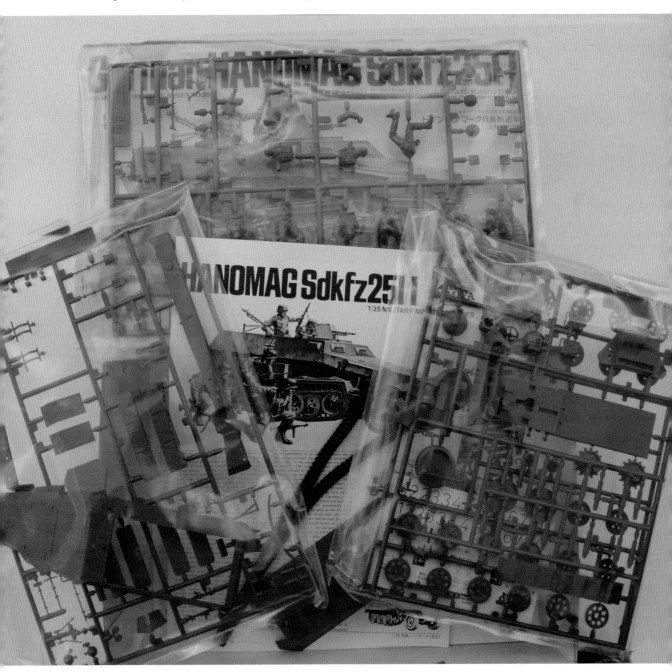

Tamiya's SdKfz 251 Ausf C – parts sprues in the box.

The completed Tamiya Pz IV Ausf D.

Tank (Tamiya Pz IV Ausf D)

As an example of a larger scale tank kit and with an eye on budget for beginners, I would recommend another Tamiya model, the Pz IV Ausf D. Again, it is an older model, but still readily available for a value price. It captures the character of the vehicle and its use during the early Blitzkrieg era. The kit includes the crew figures, depicting them wearing the distinctive black Panzer uniforms, plus the protective tanker's headgear that outwardly looks like a beret. As well as being inexpensive, it is a relatively straightforward kit to build, making it a good starter for the new modeller and for those on a limited budget.

THE HUGE SCOPE OF GERMAN AFV MODELS

My aim here is not to tell you how to build any particular model or in any particular style. What I want to touch on in this section is the vast array of German AFV models that are available, in all sorts of scales. I often hear from modellers who only build to a particular scale or a particular subject. There is nothing wrong with this, of course, but I would like to show just how much is available across the board, so that you can choose what to have a go at, be it for simple collecting or for wargaming, and with regard to different levels of skill, size (which affects your available storage and work space) and suitability for age, possibly any disabilities, and budget. There is no specific sequence, just a look at some of the large range of German AFVs, without even touching on soft-skin and horse-drawn transport. The marketplace is so vastly different to what it was when I started modelling over fifty years ago, so that now we are faced with an almost bewildering breadth of choice available to us.

Let's begin with a subject that got me started into German half-tracks, in particular the SdKfz 251, a topic which in itself could be a theme for a collection. Back then, there were no kits of it available and the idea of scratch-building all those angled plates put me off from even trying. I was so pleased when I discovered my first resin model, an SdKfz 251/1 Ausf C moulded in a polyester resin by Eric Clark. It was a one-piece body plus the two front wheels. In those very early resin models you had to provide your own axles and gun barrels. A bit later, Fujimi did the Ausf B, which had the option to make it as the basic 251/1 APC, or as the 251/10 with the 3.7cm Pak 36 mounted on top of the cab. Then there was Matchbox with its 1/76 Ausf B and later ESCI with a couple of variants, though in 1/72. In larger scale, Tamiya released its 1/35 early Ausf C, following this up with later Ausf D variants. The availability of kits for the 251 has exploded since then, with even more variants and super levels of detail from both Dragon Models and AFV Club. As a subject, it even tempted Hasegawa back to its small-scale series of 1/72 armour models after many years of stagnation, with some lovely 1/72 Ausf D variants.

For the growing wargames market, the Plastic Soldier Company has done both 15mm scale and 1/72 kits of the 251, which offer the options to build multiple variants. Most recently a Polish manufacturer, First to Fight, has been releasing 1/72 models of vehicles from the early period of World War II and among them is the early SdKfz 251 Ausf A. So far, there are the basic APC version and a Command variant, but these early Ausf As are notable for having extra vision ports down the sides of the crew compartment, a feature which was deleted from all later variants. And that is without considering all the resin kits and conversions that have been made in both large and small scales. With so many kits available now, it is little wonder that the 251 series remains a popular subject in its own right.

The 1/72 Sdkfz 251 Ausf A from First to Fight.

A selection of small-scale SdKfz 251 Ausf D variants.

One of Tamiya's more recent releases, the 1/35 Elefant.

Those early Airfix kits were very much aimed at the children's toy market, not the adult modeller. The cost of researching and tooling a model back in the 1960s was a significant investment, and it relied on sales of tens of thousands of kits. A similar approach applied to the early Tamiya kits, which featured motorized remote-control models. That's not radio control, which came later, but models with a corded connection to a battery-operated remote-control handset. That then developed with the removal of the motorization features and the change in marketing towards static models. Signs of those motorization features can still be found with holes in the bottom of the hull of a number of the older Tamiya kits. Motorization did resurface in the World War I British Mk IV tank, but it received a mixed reaction amongst modellers. Throughout the years, Tamiya has retained its reputation for well-detailed models that always build well. While staying with the provision of one-piece vinyl tracks, Tamiya offered the option of separate upgrade parts, such as etched detailing and single-link tracks. This has kept the kit

price under control, while allowing the modeller who wanted to add that extra level of detail to be able to do so. Tamiya kits have been at the heart of AFV modelling since its first kits, though its release rate for new models is not as great as that of some of its competitors.

It would be fair to describe the arrival of Dragon Models on to the market as a significant game changer, particularly for the German AFV modeller. Dragon's earliest kits were actually modern Soviet vehicles, subjects pretty much ignored up to that time. It then moved on to World War II subjects and today the variety of models includes subjects I simply never imagined we would see. So many, in fact, that it is difficult to know where to start, but a good model, which represents much of the company's innovation, is its 1/35 kit of famed German tank commander Michael Wittman's Tiger I. It is not just a case of providing the appropriate markings, it also has etched-brass detailing and a moulded-on *Zimmerit* coating, a paste-like substance that was applied to mid- to late-war German AVFs as a defence against magnetic anti-tank mines.

Dragon's 1/35 kit of Wittman's Tiger I. DRAGON MODELS

Two Dragon 1/72 Pz IIIs.

There are so many Dragon kits I could mention, but its series of Panzer III kits is certainly one to include. In my youth I had to convert the old Airfix StuG III by altering the superstructure and scratch-building a turret in order to add a Pz III to my collection. Dragon has been through pretty much every variant from early to late in not only 1/35, but 1/72 models as well.

Within this series, though, is one model that I never imagined we would see available as a plastic kit, released in Dragon's Cyber-Hobby series of kits. Early in World War II, with the prospect of an invasion of the UK ahead, the German military developed a variant of the Pz III that could be driven underwater, the 3.7cm-armed Pz III (T) Ausf F. The (T) designation stood for Tauchpanzer – Diving Tank. The German military did not build shallow-draught landing craft like those of the Allies – the bulk of its invasion craft for Operation *Sea Lion*, the planned invasion of the UK, would have been European river barges, converted with bow ramps. These would not have been able to get high up on the shore, so tanks would have had to be unloaded in deeper water. The Germans also developed a wading version of the Pz III F. It was to

have a floating snorkel to allow air to get into the engine while the vehicle was sealed and to enable it to drive along the seabed if launched a way out from the shore. It could operate at depths up to 15m and was successfully tested. It was the same basic idea as the DD Sherman, but done in a different way. The invasion never happened, but the tanks were modified to work at a shallower depth, with a short 3.5m snorkel, and were later used in river-crossing operations on the Eastern Front at the River Bug. Using its flexible DS Styrene to produce the canvas covers and flexible air tubes, Dragon added the Tauchpanzer to the range of plastic kits on sale.

Dragon's designers have increasingly added more detail to their kits over the years. It is not uncommon for them to provide two variations on the parts for the on-vehicle tools, one with moulded-on brackets and another without, as well as including etched-brass parts for you to make up the brackets. In terms of detail, the brass ones do look good, but they are a bit fiddly to make up. If you can manage them, great, but otherwise the moulded-on brackets are easier for a lot of modellers. A topic that generates discussion is the provision of single-link tracks. At the outset, these were moulded as multiple parts on sprues, which

The Dragon Cyber-Hobby kit of the Pz III Tauchpanzer.

take time to cut off and then clean up the feed points. Next step was to include 'Magic Tracks', which have the individual links supplied loose in small poly bags, usually one bag for each track. Then Dragon reverted to providing one-piece tracks, made in DS Styrene. This change suggests that these sell better than those with individual links. The detail on the DS Styrene is neat and crisp and they accept paint well. A manufacturer is inevitably influenced by sales figures when it comes to what it can continue to produce.

Over the years there has been criticism of some of Dragon's kits, with errors and some poorly pre-sented assembly instructions. Despite any of that, I applaud them for their innovation and for producing kits that we would not otherwise have seen become available. Let's consider another example, one from Dragon's Cyber-Hobby series, the mine-roller equipped variant of the Pz II. A real-life field conversion, engineers in North Africa added some mine rollers on to the front of a Pz II Ausf C. There are photos of it, but it was rather a rare beast. The Pz II Ausf C is the basic gun tank and is one of those Dragon kits which features interior detailing, with transmission and fighting compartment plus all the fittings inside the turret.

There are a few vehicles which hold an interesting connection and it is those associated with

A detail view of the Pz III Tauchpanzer.
DRAGON MODELS

Box art showing the DAK Pz II Ausf C with mine rollers.

rockets. The German military used a variety of vehicle-mounted rocket launchers. They all used rocket motors fitted in an angled ring, which induced a spin on the rocket to stabilize it in the same way rifling did for an artillery round. The smallest was the 15cm Nebelwerfer, which was fitted to a six-barrelled towed launcher, often referred to as 'moaning minnies' due to the sound they made, and a weapon my father certainly remembered from his own experiences of being on the receiving end of them. There was also vehicle mounted launcher fitted to the Panzerwerfer 42. An armoured body was fitted to the half-tracked Opel Maultier ('Mule') chassis. Between 1943–5, there were 300 of these built, along with a similar number of unarmed ammunition carriers, the Munitionskraftwagen, which was the same but simply without the launch unit. Within the armoured body wooden racks held the spare rounds. There is an excellent example of a preserved one in the collection of the Musée des Blindés at Saumur. Italeri does a neat model of it in 1/35 and there are resin models in the smaller scales as well. At the end of the war there was a similar Nebelwerfer mounting on the SWS (Schwerer Wehrmacht Schlepper) with an armoured body, and Great Wall Hobby has a well-detailed 1/35 kit of it, now marketed under the Bronco brand. There was also a 1/72 kit from Maco of this SWS variant, recently re-released within the Revell range. The next size of rockets was known as the Wurfrahmen 40. These included the 28cm HE and 32cm Incendiary, which were launched using their transport crates. Six could be mounted in frames on an SdKfz 251, known as the 'Stuka zu Fus' ('Stuka on foot') and they were also fitted to the small Renault UE carrier, a small French tractor captured in large numbers in 1940. These could carry two on each side, on a smaller frame similar to that used on the larger 251. Another variation had four mounted on a simple frame on the back of the little load carrier. Another French vehicle, the Hotchkiss H35 light tank, was also used to mount two on each side.

The biggest of them all, however, was the Sturmtiger ('Assault Tiger'), officially the Sturmmorserwagen 606/4 mit 38cm RW61. The large gun was mounted in a fixed casemate fitted to the hull of the late Tiger I. Designed as a result of experiences in city fighting on the Eastern Front, it was intended to be able to demolish whole buildings in urban combat. Just nineteen were made. Their armament was a 38cm rocket, the launcher adapted from a Kriegsmarine depth

Three alternative models of the Sturmtiger: 1/100 by Zvezda; 1/87 by Minitanks; and 1/72 by Dragon.

charge thrower. Breech-loaded, they could not vent the gases into the crew compartment, so they were vented through tubes that had their outlets around the muzzle of the launcher, giving them a very distinctive appearance. They also had a small crane fitted on the back of the casemate to assist with loading the heavy rounds of ammunition. The only urban combat use was in Warsaw and the rest were used mainly on the Western Front during the final stages of the war. Italeri has done a good 1/35 kit of the Sturmtiger, while there are also smaller scale models available in 1/72 from Dragon and 1/100 by Zvezda. At the time of writing, there is due to be a new kit set for release by Rye Field Models which will also include interior detail for the fighting compartment.

Let's take a step back for a moment. The period of the greatest successes for the German army in World War II was 1939–42. For me, two things mark that out. The first is that the standard overall colour of Panzer Grey was used throughout the period and the second is that these successes were achieved with a large proportion of small,

light tanks being involved, with the heaviest use being the Pz IV. To bolster the Panzer units, they also made good use of additional tanks which they had acquired as a result of their victories. Perhaps the best known of these was the Czech-built Pz 38(t). Only armed with a 4.7cm gun, it proved to be a very adaptable chassis that went on to be used for a variety of other gun platforms. The Pz I and II were still in front-line service in 1941 when the invasion of Russia, Operation *Barbarossa*, was launched. The Pz I was still only armed with two machine guns and the Pz II's main gun was just 2cm. The medium tank, the Pz III, was armed with a gun not much larger, just 3.7cm, while later variants had a short 5cm weapon. Even the early variants of the StuG III that were in service at this time were fitted with a low-velocity 7.5cm StuK 37 L/24 gun. They were used in the infantry-support role. It was not until 1942 that the StuG was first equipped with a high-velocity 7.5cm StuK 40 L/43 main gun and later in the same year with the slightly longer 7.5cm StuK 40 L/48 gun. These were fitted as a result of the experience of

Tamiya's 1/48 Pz 38(t).

The Pz I Ausf B Ladungsleger from Dragon Models.
DRAGON MODELS

meeting the heavier KV-1 and T-34 tanks on the Eastern Front. The slightly heavier Pz IV had the larger 7.5cm gun, but again only a short-barrelled variant before the Ausf F 2 came along with a long-barrelled version. This one saw action in North Africa, where it was known to the British as the 'Mk IV Special'.

There is a good selection of models available for this early period. My earliest recollections are kits of the Pz I Ausf B and the Pz 38(t) in 1/76 by Fujimi, and these were followed by 1/72 kits from ESCI, who also did the Pz 35(t). Moving up a notch, Tamiya has added a Pz 38(t) to its 1/48 range and done a very nice job of it.

Dragon also has a number of early war period subjects in its range, including the Pz I, II and III as well as early StuG variants and the 38(t). One slightly more unusual variant is the Pz I Ausf B Ladungsleger, a demolition charge layer with a 50kg charge. There were two variations, one with a frame that laid the charge behind the tank, while the second is the one Dragon has done, with a tubular frame that could be pivoted over the top of the tank to lay the charge in front of it.

Staying with models of the early Panzers, Bronco Models has an interesting selection in its range of 1/35 kits. Bronco's kits tend to be very highly detailed, with lots of small detail parts and individual link tracks. As well as things like the Kfz 13 armoured and the radio-equipped version

the Kfz 14, there are also two versions of the Pz 35(t), the gun tank and the radio-equipped Panzerbefehlswagen. A recent addition has been the Pz III Ausf A, which will be different for any collection of Pz III variants as it has the five larger road wheels, a design which was replaced with the smaller six-wheel arrangement on all the later versions.

Three others in the Bronco range from this period which I find interesting are those based around the Pz II Ausf D, again with large road wheels so different from the other Pz II variants. There is the basic gun tank, armed with just a 2cm gun as the main armament, plus a Brückenleger. The third variation had a slightly smaller turret armed with just a machine gun while adding two small flame projectors mounted on the track guards on either side, just above the drive sprockets. To add a bit of extra interest to this one, also included is a small tracked trailer taken from a French UE Infantry carrier, which could be used to carry drums of extra fuel for the flame guns. Again, these are subjects that years ago I never expected to see done as a plastic kit. I am now at the point where I have given up dreaming of such and such a subject, as it will most likely come along anyway.

Talking about these early war vehicles gives me a chance to move on to another specific type of tracked AFV. Most of the German anti-

Bronco's Pz II Ausf D.

Fujimi kit of the Panzerjäger I in 1/76.

tank weapons in those early stages were towed guns. The 3.7cm PaK 36, the 5cm PaK 38 and the 7.5cm PaK 40 all come to mind, but what battle experience taught was a need for a self-propelled mounting for an anti-tank weapon, the Panzerjäger. This came to be the 4.7cm PaK (t) L/43.4 Panzerjäger I. This fitted the Czech-made gun without its carriage on the hull of a Pz I Ausf B, which had the turret removed and a taller gun shield open at the back. While it saw service in 1940–42, it had been phased out by 1943. Kits are available in 1/76, 1/72 and 1/35 scales. It helped to establish the requirement for a self-propelled anti-tank gun mounting that offered some protection to the crew and increased the mobility of the weapon as well. The difference in what was to come was marked by the general increase in the size and weight of the guns that they carried.

The Panzerjäger enabled the German army to make use of those older tank chassis which had turrets that were not big enough to take larger guns. However, if the turret was taken off and the hull opened up, a larger gun could be carried. Not only did this save wasting a useful chassis, without the complexities of including a turret in production they could be built relative quickly. Even the guns that were fitted made best use of their resources. With so many captured guns from initial successes on the Eastern Front, a lot of these were fitted to the Panzerjäger, in particular the Russian 7.62cm PaK 36(r). Fitted to the Pz II Ausf D chassis, these were known as the Marder II. When atop a Pz

38(t) hull, it was one of three variations referred to as the Marder III, a second version of which had the German 7.5cm PaK 40/3 fitted in a different style of gun shield, though still open-backed. A third version, the Ausf M, used the same weapon, but had a significant change to the hull as the engine was moved from the back to a central position and the rear section of the hull used to create the crew compartment, where they had good space to serve the gun. Nearly 1,000 examples of the Ausf M were built between 1943–4. It was eventually superseded on the production lines by the low-profile Hetzer. The same Ausf M hull was also used to mount the 15cm sIG33/2 heavy infantry gun, of which over 280 were built. Kits of all of these are available in both large and small scales. While Dragon and Tamiya have Marders in 1/35 scale, smaller examples are made by the Plastic Soldier Company in both 15mm and 1/72 scales, while ESCI also did a couple of kits in its 1/72 range, now part of the Italeri label. Because the open fighting compartments contain plenty of things like ammunition stowage and radios as well as the workings of the gun itself, there is plenty of visual interest in these Panzerjäger for the modeller to focus on. The other one just to make quick mention of is the Marder I, which had the 7.5cm PaK 40/1 mounted inside an armoured superstructure fitted to the stock of a captured French Lorraine Schlepper load carrier.

Staying with the topic of these open-top self-propelled guns comes the Hornisse, or Nashorn.

A selection of various small-scale Marders.

The long-barrelled Hornisse/Nashorn in 1/72.

Using the Pz IV chassis, it carried the large and very powerful 8.8cm Pak 43/1 L/71. This long-barrelled gun was one of the most powerful anti-tank weapons of the war and is instantly recognizable by the very long barrel. There are some neat kits of this available in both 1/72 (from Revell and Dragon), as well as 1/35 (Dragon and AFV Club). The same chassis, with mid-mounted engine and fighting compartment at the back end, was also used to carry the 15cm Sfh18/1 L/30, kits of which are also available.

Then there were the Jagdpanzers ('Tank Hunters'). These were fully enclosed armoured superstructures on various types of tank chassis. Small and low, there was the 7.5cm-armed Hetzer, based on the Pz 38(t) chassis built by Skoda. It is a popular model subject, available in both large and small scales. On the Pz IV chassis there were three variations of the Jagdpanzer IV. The first had a low, fixed superstructure of well-sloped armour plates and the vertical front plate of the hull was replaced by a pointed nose from two sharply angled plates. Armed with a 7.5cm PaK 39 L/48, it is commonly recognized for the barrel being fitted with a muzzle brake. This was followed by the Panzer IV/70(V), which was fitted

with the longer barrelled 7.5cm PaK 42 L/70. This one is notable for having the longer gun barrel without a muzzle brake and being slightly more nose-heavy, which caused excessive wear to the front two road wheels on each side, so that these were usually replaced with steel-rimmed wheels. Another notable fitting to the later versions was the inclusion of the Vorsatz-P mount in the roof. This was for local defence and involved a mount for the 7.92mm MP44 machine pistol, fitted with a curved barrel attachment. Over 900 of these were built before the end of the war.

The third version was the Panzer IV/70(A). This also carried the larger 7.5cm PaK 42 L/70, but with the superstructure not so heavily sloped and fitted directly to the normal Ausf J hull, although with the bottom section of the superstructure vertical and extended out to the edge of the track guards. It is taller than the other two variants, but with the same nose-heavy problem that required the two front wheel stations to have steel-rimmed wheels fitted. Kits of all of these are available. There are plenty of wartime photos showing one captured in France and this vehicle is preserved and on display at the French armour museum in Saumur. Extra interest is that

Jagdpanzer IV/70V. DRAGON MODELS

My early build of the Fujimi Elefant. My first full scratchbuilt model, done when I was in my early teens.

the museum has another Jagdpanzer IV there as well and the difference in size between the two versions is instantly apparent.

This leads on to three more large and powerful Jagdpanzers. The Elefant made use of some chassis that were built for Porsche's design for the Tiger (P), while the competing Tiger (H) was selected for production. The ninety Porsche chassis were built with a fixed armoured casemate and carried the 8.8cm PaK 43/2 L/71. Heavily armoured, these saw action first at Kursk in 1943, where a number of losses were sustained, which identified the need to fit a machine gun for defence against infantry attack. Various kits are available, the most recent being from Tamiya.

Even bigger, though, was the Jagdtiger, built on an extended Tiger II hull, which carried the much larger 12.8cm gun, the PaK 44 L/55. This was another piece of evidence of the rapidly increasing size of both weapons and vehicles during the later stages of the war. Kits are available in both large and small scales. In its 1/35 range, Dragon has even done one portraying the rare Porsche suspension seen on the preserved example at Bovington.

Staying with a late-war theme, which demonstrates one of the significant changes as the war progressed, was the need for armoured self-propelled anti-aircraft weapons. During the Blitzkrieg era, the Luftwaffe protected the advancing German units from enemy air attacks using specialist support aircraft such as the Stuka, and the air force, infantry and armoured units worked well together as a combined-arms force. As the war progressed, however, the quality and quantity of Allied air power proved an ever more dangerous threat. As a result, there was a marked increase in the provision of mobile anti-aircraft weapons deployed with the Panzer units. The Pz IV chassis provided the Möbelwagen ('Removal Van'), which had four flat armoured plates that folded down to provide a working platform for the crew of a 2cm Flakvierling quad mounting. It was also used to mount the single-barrelled 3.7cm FlaK 43 L/60. These did still expose the gun crew to attack, so there were also two turreted designs, the Wirbelwind with the quad 2cm Flakvierling 38 and the Ostwind, which carried the 3.7cm FlaK 43/1 L/60. The Pz IV also provided the chassis

The old Fujimi 1/76 kit of the Jagdtiger has stood the test of time well.

Dragon 1/35 Ostwind. DRAGON MODELS

Dragon 1/35 Wirbelwind. DRAGON MODELS

Dragon's 1/35 SdKfz 7 Flakvierling with armoured cab.
DRAGON MODELS

The smaller scale version, very nicely done in 1/72 by Revell.

for the Kugelblitz, a twin 3cm MK103/38 in an armoured sphere contained within the low turret. Only two were actually completed, but it is still available in kit form.

The 2cm Flakvierling and the 3.7cm FlaK were also fitted on the back of the SdKfz 7 half-track. Fold-down sides provided the crew with a working platform and enabled the weapons to have a full 360-degree traverse. Armoured protection was added for the crew cab. While both Trumpeter and Dragon have some excellent models of these in 1/35, Revell has also done some equally good models in 1/72. A further development late in the war was the use of the armoured version of the SWS half-track. This has been done by Great Wall Hobby, though these are now available under the Bronco label.

There is another category of vehicle to mention. In the early stages of the war there was a variety of armoured cars, some with four, some with six wheels (six-rad) and some with eight (eight-rad). As the war progressed, the eight-rad armoured car range developed. Used particularly by reconnaissance units, they had driving positions at each end, so that they could be driven equally quickly both backwards and forwards. The old Airfix kit of the SdKfz 234 back in the 1960s had a number of faults, but nowadays there are excellent and highly detailed 1/35 models by Italeri, Dragon and AFV Club. In the smaller 1/72 scale, Dragon has done a couple, while Hasegawa has also returned to its 1/72 armour range with a couple of excellent kits. Most recently, and with the wargamer in mind, the Plastic Soldier Company has done kits in both 15mm scale and the larger 1/72, which provide multiple kits in the box and options to build them in your choice of variants. The point about this series of vehicles is that they were the only eight-wheel armoured cars in use during World War II, yet since the war many other nations have also been deploying eight-wheel vehicles, such as the Soviet BTR-60, -70 and -80 series, the American LAV and Stryker and the modern German GTK Boxer.

Examples of the small four-wheel SdKfz 222 and radio-equipped SdKfz 223.

So, there are plenty of different types of German AFVs from World War II and models widely available across different scales. An interesting variety of other armoured vehicles was also built, but only in prototype form or in limited numbers, such as the schwerer Minenraumer, which Takom has done in 1/35, a huge experimental mine exploder found in Germany by US forces at the end of the war. An armoured version of the amphibious tractor, the Landwasserschlepper, has been done by Dragon in both 1/35 and 1/72 kits, which provide both the prototypes and the differences between them, plus a floating bridge bay that would have been slung between them and used as a vehicle ferry. Particularly interesting is the Ersatz M10 Panther, a Panther tank disguised with sheet metal panels, painted in Olive Drab and given US markings to look like a US M10 tank destroyer at first sight. It was used during the Ardennes Offensive in December 1944, when it was intended to deceive and confuse US forces until it was too late. Most were actually identified and knocked out, but it makes for an interesting model and a very different looking Panther.

Other oddities that come to mind include the little one-man tank design, the Kugelpanzer ('Ball Tank'). At least one of these was actually built and resides in the Russian collection at Kubinka. There is a 1/72 resin model of it in the range from Attack Hobby Kits in the Czech Republic. Another oddity was the wheel-cum-track armoured observation post vehicle used in North Africa, the Mittlerer Gepanzerter Beobachungsfraftwagen SdKfz 254, which is kitted in 1/35 by HobbyBoss and as a metal model in 1/72 by SHQ.

If you have the space, there is one other style of armoured vehicle that is available – armoured trains, which were used mainly on the Eastern Front. Trumpeter does a range of these in 1/35, including the armoured locomotive and the various artillery, Command, infantry and AA cars. There is a fair cost to each one and the assembled models will take up a lot of display space if you want to build up a full train. If you have less space, just recently HobbyBoss has released the BR57 Armoured Loco in 1/72, so perhaps the company will also scale down the armoured rail cars from the Trumpeter range. The alternative will be the resin models originally done by Model Transport, which are now under the Matador Models banner. The smaller Panzerdrazine rail cars are also available in scales varying from 1/144, to 1/72 and 1/35.

The large 1/35 Raumer-S, a Takom kit.

Dragon's 1/72 Landwasserschlepper prototypes I and II and Fahrendeck.

Panther Ersatz M10 in 1/72.

The little Kugelpanzer in 1/72 from Attack Hobby.

There is one other group of models that I feel should be included. These are the ready built and painted examples of their kits by Dragon, Modelcollect, Trumpeter and Zvezda. They are generally very nicely done and presented in plastic display cases, and available in the various colours and marking options provided in their kits. As well as for collectors, these are good for youngsters who may then feel they would like to have a go at making their own. Equally, they are good for the older enthusiast who might be experiencing problems with eyesight and dexterity that make it difficult to build their own models as time goes on. These ready built models would still allow them to add to their collections and continue to enjoy and take part in our hobby.

The Mittlerer Gepanzerter Beobachtungsfraftwagen SdKfz 254 from SHQ.

Pre-built King Tigers in 1/72 in the Dragon Armour range.

Panthers and the Hornisse/Nashorn by Dragon Armour.

Another development that has been gaining ever more traction with manufacturers is the increasing number of simplified kits aimed at the wargames market. The likes of S-Model, Italeri, Armourfast andTthe Plastic Soldier Company all have kits with two or more complete models in the box. The tracked vehicles have simplified track and running gear units, so they are quick to assemble. Dragon has released the Pxz IV Ausf D in 1/72, which features the track, road wheels and return rollers moulded in one-piece black soft vinyl, quite a departure from the level of individual road wheels in its earlier Pz IV kits. Some will like these developments, others will not, but the implication of the level of development going into this style of model indicates that there is a significant market for them and, put simply, they clearly sell well enough to encourage so many companies to follow the format.

*Dragon's new 1/72
Pz IV Ausf D with the
simplified running gear.*

*Armourfast
1/72 StuIG 33B.*

15mm-scale Pz IIIs by The Plastic Soldier Company.

THE PzKpfw V PANTHER

The Panther came about largely as a result of the German experiences on the Eastern Front, following the invasion of Russia in 1941, when the appearance of the Soviet T-34/76 came as something of a surprise. A requirement for a new tank in the 30-ton class was issued and both Daimler-Benz and MAN competed for the chassis design, while Rheinmetall-Borsig was responsible for the turret. The result was that MAN was given the production orders, to start in 1942 for operational deployment beginning in 1943, when the Panthers saw action in the Kursk battles. The eventual design weighed in at a hefty 43 tons.

The first one to see service was, oddly, the Ausf D; the Ausf A came later. The third series was the Ausf G, of which over 3,000 were built between 1944 and 1945. Just like the Tiger, the later versions were fitted with steel wheels due to the shortage of rubber. They were visually all very similar, although the early Ausf D had a simpler, 'dustbin-shaped' cupola. The Ds and some As had a thin flap on the front right of the hull to allow for firing a hull machine gun. This was replaced on later As and the G with a ball-mounted hull machine gun. The G also had a straight edge to the dull sides as well. The Panther F, which would have had a smaller Schmalturm turret, never went into production. An example of the prototype turret, or at least the shattered remains of it, is on display at the Tank museum. A single prototype Panther II hull was completed before the end of the war, and this is preserved at Fort Benning in the USA, after many years at Fort Knox.

The Panther was also used as a Command version, the Panzerbefehlswagen and an Observation version, the Panzer Beobachtungswagen, which had the main gun removed and a dummy barrel fitted to the front of the turret, plus a ball-mounted machine gun. It left more room for a plotting table and other equipment within the turret space. Other production variants were the Jagdpanther, with just under 400 built, with the powerful 8.8cm PaK 43/3 L/71 gun in a fixed armoured superstructure. The other major variant was a dedicated recovery version, the Bergepanther. Other projects planned, such as turreted AA gun mounts, remained only as a wooden mock-up or paper designs that were halted by the end of the war.

Chapter Six

Painting and Weathering

GERMAN AFV COLOURS

The following will not be a complete guide to German AFV colours of World War II, but simply enough to give a modeller an idea of the basics, with more references provided in the Bibliography at the end of the book. At the outset of World War II, the German armed forces used a plain single coat of a very dark grey, Panzer Grey, along with a few still in pre-war camouflage using Panzer Grey combined with disruptive schemes of brown and/ or dark green. The interior of the Panzers was an ivory white in the crew compartment, though other colours featured on internal fittings and elements such as transmissions, gearbox, engine and so on. The almost white colour was useful to help reflect the limited light within an enclosed AFV. For open-top vehicles, such as half-tracks and armoured cars, the interior was the same colour as the exterior; a lighter shade would have made them too easy to spot from the air.

An interesting variation came when the Panzers went to North Africa, as they were generally shipped out there still in Panzer Grey, but had the sand-brown camouflage colour painted over the external surfaces once they were there. What was often found, though, was that interiors of half-tracks were often left in the dark grey, giving an interesting combination for the modeller. The sand-brown paint, a shade sometimes referred to as Afrika Korps Desert Yellow, was quite easily worn, both by crew access and simply from the effects of the abrasive wind-blown sand. That heavily worn finish provides something of a challenge for modellers, as the base coat of dark grey would show through.

The other temporary paint that wore quite heavily was the winter white colour applied particularly on the Eastern Front. Again, the grey base coat would show through, as the white was a temporary whitewash, often applied locally by individual vehicle crews in the field, sometimes with things as simple as a broom, or a handful of straw. The white paint was also in short supply at some points, so paint was sometimes applied sparingly without complete coverage, In some instances, it was just a case of draping white sheets 'liberated' from the local population to try to prevent the dark grey machines from standing out in the snow-covered countryside. As the white paint wore, and was added to by mud from thawing snow, the colours blended more into the surroundings.

In 1943, there was a major change, as new vehicles coming out of the factory and others coming from major maintenance were painted in an overall colour Dunkelgelb (dark yellow) and each vehicle was also supplied with tins of paint paste, with Dunkelgrun (dark green) and Rot-Brun (red-brown). These were to allow the individual crews or units to apply them as appropriate to the area in which they were in action. The paste could be thinned with water, though that wore off quite easily, and a more permanent solution was to thin it with petrol. As the war went on, though, fuel supplies became under pressure, so that to use it to thin paint was seen as being rather wasteful of a valuable resource. Many units did have their maintenance units apply common patterns to their equipment and these would use spray guns to apply some elaborate patterns.

In the modellers' world, there has been a great deal of discussion over the years about what are the 'correct' shades of these colours. In reality, the colour will have depended on how much thinner was used and whether it was sprayed on or brush-painted. The effects of weather and age also need to be taken into account, with the result that, in my view, if it 'looks' right, that is all you need to worry about. Unlike modellers, most fighting soldiers would have not worried about whether their equipment all had matching shades of paint. Even different batches of that original paste from different manufacturers would have resulted in plenty of extra variation over time. In the final stages of the war, the base colour used for equipment coming out of the factories changed once more, as the vehicles emerged in an overall colour of a rust-coloured primer and then had camouflage colours added as required by different units. What you will gather from this is that provided the basics are followed between the early and late periods of the war, exact shades were pretty much infinitely variable, as were the variety of camouflage patterns employed. A few exceptions also appeared, with some standard factory applied-colour schemes, such as some late-war patterns used on Hetzers from the Skoda factory.

One particular scheme to mention is referred to as the 'Ambush' scheme. This used the same basic colours in disruptive patterns of the three late-war colours, but with the addition of small spots of Dunkelgelb on the Dunkelgrun and Rot-Brun, and Dunkelgrun and Rot-Brun on Dunkelgelb. The idea was to represent the kind of dappled light that comes through trees, so that a gun might be positioned in the Ambush position amongst trees waiting for an enemy tank to approach. The scheme was used on a wide variety of vehicles, though the one that strikes me as the most appropriate was the small, low-profiled Hetzer.

PAINTING THE MODELS

It's now time to move on to painting the models.

KFfz 13

As this is an early war piece of kit, I gave it an overall colour of Panzer Grey, applied using a spray can, or 'rattle can', one of the colours in the Tank Warsprays cans by the Plastic Soldier Company.

Model with the overall coat of Panzer Grey paint.

The completed Kfz 13 with transfers applied.

There are five different Tank Warsprays – Panzer Grey and Dunkelgelb, as well as other basic colours for Russian Green, US Olive Drab and UK Khaki Drab. These are good paints that work well and come in larger cans than many other manufacturers', so are good value for money.

I prefer to use these sprays outdoors or in my garden shed, so that the smell doesn't make me unpopular inside the house. They also dry very quickly, so you can use a light spray, let it dry, then do another layer to build up the coverage. If you apply too much in one go, it may pool and run, a potential issue using any spray cans or airbrushes.

Let it dry thoroughly, about twenty-four hours, then start brush-painting the details which in this case are simply the seats, the MG34, the canvas cover for the spare wheel and the tyres. In the pre-war days when KFfz 13s were built, leather would have likely been used for the seat, hence the colour. Later in the war it would have been canvas. The gun is a dark Gun Metal or Satin Black, which captures the real colour of the MG. Finally, it is just a case of applying the transfers supplied in the kit and using some pigments to create light weathering.

StuG III Ausf A

With metal and resin models, the first thing is to give them a coat of primer. There is a wide variety available, but I use the large aerosol cans of grey or white acrylic primer from Halfords as they work well, are readily available and reasonably priced. Let that dry for twenty-four hours. Once that is dry, apply another spray-can finish of Panzer Grey.

The tracks need to be painted, along with the road wheel tyres and the stowed tools. For these

The model with an overall coat of primer.

The model with an overall coat of Panzer Grey.

A completed StuG Ausf A. To be honest, though, this is another model to the one I was building, as I had a disaster with that and it was irreparably broken – it happens to us all at some point.

kits you need to source some markings, either from your spares box or one of the various after-market suppliers.

SdKfz 251/17 Ausf C

Once finished, this model requires a coat of primer. I opted for the later war colours of

Dunkelgelb (simply applied from a spray can), then brush-painted the tracks, road wheel tyres and camouflage scheme. Though I did not add them, there is a set of crew figures for this one available in the Milicast range.

Primed model.

Base coat of Dunkelgelb.

The completed model.

Jagdpanzer E100

We left this with a basic coat of Dunkelgelb. Firstly, I applied a dark track wash to the tracks once they were in place.

As these tanks were never actually built, you can suit yourself with the pattern of your late-war camouflage. I chose to airbrush a green and brown pattern, using paints by Mission Models. Once dry, the whole model was brushed with a tan filter for these German three-colour schemes by AMMO of Mig Jiminez (other manufacturers also do one that is similar).

With that done and transfers applied, the model is lightly weathered using pigments. A Tamiya weathering pigment of Light Sand is brushed on to highlight all the edges of superstructure, hatches and so on. An AMMO products Dark Earth pigment was then applied to the running gear and tracks before the thicker liquid of AMMO Turned Earth was brushed onto the lower hull and bottom edges of the track guards to simulate mud splashed up by movement. The final touch was to rub a Gun Metal pigment (alternatively, powdered graphite works well) on to the track links where they would be worn when driving the vehicle on roads. With that, this model is wrapped up.

Track wash is applied to the track of the Jagdpanzer.

Camouflage applied, plus the tan filter and transfers.

The completed model with light weathering.

Armoured Krupp Protze
Kfz 69 with 3.7cm Pak 36

With the paintwork done, an overall Panzer Grey plus the details, it was then time to add the transfers for the markings. These are the common water-slide style markings, which you soak in water to release the individual transfer and place in position on the model. I always cut the individual markings into separate elements rather than soak everything at once. This gives more time for working and getting the positioning right for each one. When applying transfers, air bubbles can become trapped beneath them. The best way to avoid this is to apply some Humbrol Decalfix using a brush to where the transfer is to go. Next, apply the transfer and adjust to get the position right, then use a cotton bud to press it down on to the model and get rid of the excess liquid. Apply a little more Decalfix on top of the transfer and use a cotton bud again to fix it. This reliably avoids any

silvering effect (the term used to describe trapped air bubbles). The markings provided are for the national crosses, number plate, unit marking and tactical symbol, along with the tyre pressure prompts over the front and rear wheels.

With this all done, I used the Tamiya Pale Grey weathering pigment to simulate wear and highlight the edges/detail. The AMMO Turned Earth 'splashes' mud was applied to the underside of the front and rear mudguards to create the type of 'muck' you will find under the wings of your own car. Then Dark Earth pigment was applied to the central part of all the wheels (including the spares), followed by a lighter European Earth pigment on the tyre treads, access steps and around the gun platform where the crew's boots would have brought mud up on to it. That rounds off a light weathering, which can be fixed in place with a spray coat of matt varnish.

Humbrol Decalfix, brush, cotton bids and a bowl of water, ready to apply the transfers.

The model with the Tamiya Light Grey pigment to highlight details and wear.

The completed and weathered model (front).

The completed and weathered model (rear).

PAINT OPTIONS

There is a great variety of model paints on the market these days. It's very different to when I started back in the 1960s, when Humbrol was almost the only game in town. There were Airfix paints in those days, but the Humbrol enamels grew to be the market leader. They were also the first to introduce a series of Authentic Colours. Enamel paints require more aggressive thinners, such as turpentine or white spirit, to thin the paint or simply clean the brushes. You do, however, get a resilient coat of paint.

Humbrol's enamels are still available, though in recent years the range has been duplicated in water-based acrylic colours. Acrylic paints have largely taken over in recent years, as, being water-based, they avoid one having to work amidst the fumes of turps or white spirit. Acrylics are easy to use and have the benefit of a quick drying time, though this can be a disadvantage if you want to blend shades of colour. However, it is about planning your work and preparing the colours so that you can blend them as you go across a model. The number of manufacturers producing ranges of modelling paints, particularly acrylics, still seems to be something of a growth area that is difficult to keep up with.

Most manufactures of acrylic paints these days produce them in themed sets covering aircraft as well as AFVs, although most do also sell the colours individually and have an extensive range of colours. There is also a very useful variety of weathering washes, filters and effects available. You can find some very helpful 'How To' guides explaining the best ways to obtain these various effects on your models. These are freely available on the manufacturers' websites and some are included in printed catalogues as well. You can, for example, buy products to create effects such as streaking grime, fuel stains, grease and many others. These are thinned enamels and, while you could make your own, buying ready made products just makes life easier.

AMMO of Mig Jiminez paints.

With the basic paintwork done, the safe thing is to seal it with a coat of matt varnish, then apply the effect on top, so that, if necessary, the effect can be removed without having to redo the whole paint job. The basic method for most models is to paint a line of the chosen colour along the top edge of the vehicle plates, allow a short time for it to dry a bit (about twenty minutes), then use a clean brush with thinners and 'streak' the colour down (or up) the sides. The nice thing is that you can adjust it to faint or dark, depending on how you want it, or, if you take off too much, just add some more.

In applying the various filters, which are designed to go with particular colours, all over the vehicle, this helps to tie all the colours together. I always think that the Tan designed for the German three-colour camouflage works especially well. AK Interactive, AMMO of Mig Jiminez and Adam Wilder all do their own series of filters and weathering effects. Check out their websites for details of their full ranges.

AK Interactive, a Spanish-based company, has also got involved with creating the colours and marking guides for the Meng range of kits (from China), and has included some of its paint sets keyed to the Meng range. Another Spanish-based company, AMMO of Mig Jiminez, is doing the same thing with the Chinese manufacturer Takom.

If you want to create the heavily worn paint that was seen both with Winter White and Desert Sand (over a base coat of Panzer Grey), there is a technique referred to as the 'hairspray technique'. Once you have the base coat on, spray it with hairspray, then spray over that with the top colour. Rubbing on it with something like a stiff brush will create the worn effect. An alternative, which I like to use, is the Washable Agent in the range from AK Interactive. Mix that with acrylic paint for the top layer, then, using a damp brush or cotton buds, rub it down where you want the wear to be.

Another new paint range on the market is Mission Models. These paints are geared towards airbrush application, for which they are rapidly

AK Interactive paints and weathering materials.

A Marder III with winter whitewash worn using the Washable Agent.

A selection of lacquer paints from the Polish manufacturer, Hataka.

gaining a good reputation. The range of colours is still growing and they are available from various retailers in the UK and from the importers, Tiger Hobbies Ltd.

Most of the paint manufacturers offer metallic colours in a variety of shades. One of the best is Alclad, whose system is intended for airbrush application, where you apply a base coat of black and then cover it with a metallic shade. More recently, the company has started another series, Alclad II, this time with military colours, and again intended for airbrush application.

A recent addition is lacquer paints. These have been coming from Polish paint manufacturer Hataka, and most recently AK Interactive has also announced a new range of lacquer colours. I gather they are particularly good for airbrush application.

OIL PAINTS
Distributed by AK Interactive, the Abteilung 502 range is a high-quality brand of oil paints. It is a very useful paint for creating worn and weathered finishes. The advantage of using oil paints is that while they do require the use of thinners such as white spirit or turpentine, they have a long drying time, so there is plenty of time to work with them and blend colours. The Abteilung 502 colours are available as individual tubes of paint, or, as is now common, in subject-themed sets. A range of ground pigments in a wide variety of colours has been added, plus a series of good-quality paint brushes. Again, seal the basic paint with matt varnish, then apply dots of different coloured oils and use a wide brush with thinners to add streaking effects over the surface of the model.

I will just go slightly off topic for a moment and add at this point that I prefer to use oils for painting faces/flesh and on horses, where the paint looks right to my eyes for the natural sheen of a horse's coat. Thanks to their longer drying time, you will also have more time to blend the shadows and highlights.

PAINT RACKS
The more years you are a modeller, the more paints you will accumulate. I have a mix of enamels, various makes of acrylics and lacquers. I'd hate to admit just how many I have and equally would not want even to attempt to count them all. You buy a colour(s) for a particular project, then it may be unused for a long time, but meanwhile you're adding more colours for other projects and so it goes on. It is easy enough to store your paints in drawer units, but I have become a real fan of also making use of a paint rack or two for those I use most frequently. Paint racks are available in different arrangements and in different sizes, so you can choose one which is best suited for your own work area. My favourites are the ones made by Sphere Products, who make a great variety of racks and storage cubes that are laser-cut and available in different sizes to suit the bottles of different manufacturers (for example, Tamiya/Lifecolor is one size, another for Humbrol tinlets and another for Vallejo). Have a look at Sphere Colours' website (http://www.sphereproducts.co.uk/) for options and prices and they can make custom designs for you as well. If you are handy with woodwork you could make your own, but commercially available racks are a time-saver.

BRUSHES
The humble paintbrush has been around for centuries and is one of the basic tools for a modeller. They are readily available both online and in local art stores on the high street. The prices can be very variable, with the best quality being Kolinsky Sable for use with water-based paint. These are made from the tail hairs of the Kolinsky, a Siberian Weasel. The best quality hair comes from the male weasel, but most brushes are a mix of male/female hair (60:40 generally). These brushes are durable and hold their shape well.

There are many other types of brush on the market, some with natural hair and others with artificial fibres such as Nylon. These are cheaper and readily available. There are different qualities,

A selection of brushes.

so maybe ask in an art shop for some guidance on which brushes will suit your needs. Humbrol revamped its range of brushes a few years ago and I use these regularly. These are reasonably priced and widely available.

Brushes are also available in different-shaped heads and each has its own place. Round-head brushes are the ones I use most – a medium-sized one for general painting of base colours, then a variety of smaller, finer heads for more detailed work. Flat-head brushes of various sizes are also handy, though I tend to use these more for the various weathering effects and when applying thinner to 'streak' effects.

If you take care of your brushes, wash them well after each use to clean off paint residues and dry them gently on a soft cloth, they will last a reasonable amount of time. Very fine brush points can become damaged and lose their points if not treated with basic care. When not in use, it is best to keep them in the protective plastic sleeves they are usually supplied with. However, no matter how careful you are about cleaning your brushes after use, over time there will be a build-up of pigment at the top of the brush head, even though the main part and tip remain in good condition. This

is normal, as it is the head of the brush which is the 'paint reservoir' holding the paint and feeding it to the point. A handy tool developed in recent years is a cleaner called Brush Magic by Deluxe Materials here in the UK and, as the name implies, after just a short time in the liquid, it dissolves that hardened paint sediment and restores the brush head to as good as new. Brushes will eventually wear out, but don't throw them away, as they are then useful for applying things like pigments during the weathering process. Only when they are really 'too far gone' do they get binned. Brush-painting is still my most frequent method of painting my models.

SPRAY CANS

Aerosol cans of spray paint are not really for detailed work, but can be a very useful tool. They are made by a variety of manufacturers, Tamiya being perhaps the best known amongst AFV modellers. Humbrol and Revell also make a useful range of colours. There are two others, however, that I use a lot. The first is as a primer, especially for resin and metal models. For this I use the large cans of auto acrylic primer, readily available in Halfords. There

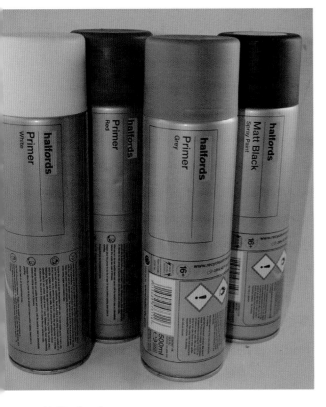

Halfords primers.

Tank Sprays from The Plastic Soldier Company.

Revell sprays.

are four colours, all of which I have used. The most common is grey, but I also have white, black and a red primer. All are matt finish paints. The other range of spray paints is quite small in terms of the number of colours, but for base coats I use them a lot. These are the Tank Sprays by the Plastic Soldier Company, which come in US Olive, British Khaki Drab, Russian Green, Panzer Grey and Dunkelgelb. These large 400ml cans provide good, consistent colours that work for plenty of models, so are good value for money. I also regularly use a couple of colours from the Revell range, which I find are very nice, although they come in small cans. I like the Matt Black and Matt Varnish in particular.

Using these aerosol cans it is vital to shake them well before use, to ensure that the pigment mixes correctly with the liquid carrier. The cans include a ball bearing inside to help that mix and this is what provides their common name of 'rattle cans'. If you can't hear the rattle, the ball is likely embedded in the pigment that has settled in the base if it has been standing unused – you must hear the rattle before proceeding to use the can.

One simple tip is to use multiple thin coats rather than trying to get full coverage in one pass. That is likely to clog detail and may run and pool around edges. Just have the patience to build up the colour gradually.

AIRBRUSHING

Another step change for armour modellers from when I started building kits to today is the use of an airbrush. However, at this point I am going to upset some by saying that an airbrush is not essential. It is a very desirable, 'nice to have' item and I enjoy using mine when I do, but it is an expensive piece of kit when combined with a compressor and it does take time and practice to become proficient. The price of an airbrush varies, as you can buy relatively cheap ones that are fine for occasional use, but for more professional modellers the better quality

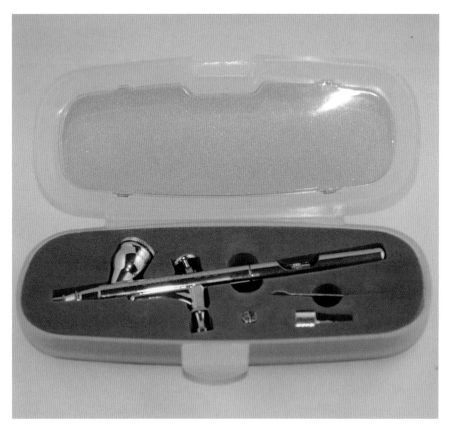

A Sparmax double-action airbrush.

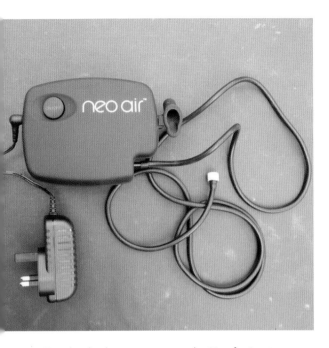

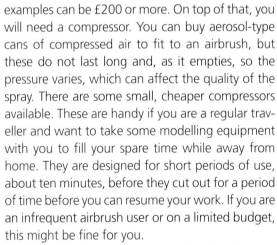

Travel or budget compressor, the Neo for Iwata.

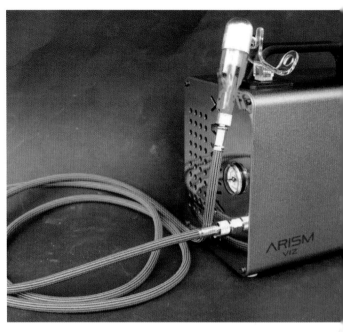

Mid-level air compressor, the Arism Viz.

examples can be £200 or more. On top of that, you will need a compressor. You can buy aerosol-type cans of compressed air to fit to an airbrush, but these do not last long and, as it empties, so the pressure varies, which can affect the quality of the spray. There are some small, cheaper compressors available. These are handy if you are a regular traveller and want to take some modelling equipment with you to fill your spare time while away from home. They are designed for short periods of use, about ten minutes, before they cut out for a period of time before you can resume your work. If you are an infrequent airbrush user or on a limited budget, this might be fine for you.

There are others at the next level, with a bit more refinement, but still with limits on time that mean they cut out before getting too hot, say around twenty minutes. The expensive compressors can be run for much longer periods of time and rather than supply a constant stream of air, they feed it into a pressure reservoir, which then passes the air through a regulator to control the pressure that goes through to the airbrush itself. As the reservoir is filled, so the pump turns itself on and off as

necessary in order to maintain just the supply in the reservoir. That in turn saves energy. So, there is a variety of airbrushes and compressors available and it is up to the individual modeller to decide which most suits their requirements. My point is that an airbrush can be an expensive tool. That's fine for the adult modeller who can afford them, but it would be such a loss if youngsters or those without the income to support a major purchase such as this were to be put off from enjoying our hobby because they didn't have an airbrush.

The most common airbrush is referred to as double-action. You press the trigger in to open the air flow from the compressor (better quality compressors let you adjust the pressure they deliver) and pull the trigger back to control the movement of the needle within the body of the brush, which regulates the flow of paint.

Any type of paint can be used in an airbrush – enamel, acrylic or lacquer. Some paints need a thinner to help keep an even paint application and to avoid the needle of the airbrush becoming clogged with pigment. In recent years, we have become spoilt by the growing range of paints that

A top-range compressor, the Smart Jet Pro from Iwata.

come ready formulated for use in an airbrush, thereby removing the guesswork about how much thinner to use to a given volume of paint. A good idea is to check the paint manufacturer's guidance for advice on thinning their paints when using an airbrush. One other tip – while acrylics can be thinned with water, manufacturers use their own chemical mix and you do get the best result from using their own brand of thinners, which are formulated to work well with their own paints. An advantage to using acrylics is that they are water-based, so it can be quick to rinse the airbrush through between using different colours. When you finish a session, it is important to give the brush a thorough clean.

I like to use an airbrush for the application of the multicolour disruptive pattern camouflage schemes, such as the late-war three-colour patterns seen on German armour, though there are still hard-edge patterns that can be applied using masks to get the harder edges to the colours, or of course you can apply by brush-painting. There

is a lot of information on building models on the Internet these days, in particular YouTube tutorials of how to do things. I sometimes see things here which detail using an airbrush for primers and base coats, which strikes me as making the process more complicated and time-consuming than it needs to be, especially if you are going to cover it with other colours and filters.

You will come across a variety of airbrushing techniques being used. Artistically they look great, but I sometimes see models which, to my mind, don't look realistic. This is most common on AFVs with a single overall colour where individual panels are highlighted and shaded. Attractive to look at, but not the flat colour you would see on the real thing. There is plenty of debate on the rights and wrongs of artistic ability and looking like the 'real thing'. Every modeller will have their own view and that means every modeller is right. Modelling is primarily for your own enjoyment and satisfaction and if it differs to someone else, that's not a problem. There are plenty of tutorials available on YouTube and on a variety of modelling sites, and I can honestly say by more talented modellers than me, so I won't add any more here. Other styles include 'Pre-shading' and 'Black and White Technique', but I have to be honest and say I don't use such techniques, feeling they add complexity to finishing a model, but that is only my opinion.

USING PIGMENTS FOR CAMOUFLAGE

Having been a long-time brush painter, I can talk about one other technique available to the non-airbrush user and that is to use green and/or red-brown pigments applied with a stiff brush (an old brush is good for this) for camouflage. Apply a base coat of paint, brush-painted or from a 'rattle can', then use an old brush to work the coloured pigments into a camouflage pattern. It takes only a little practice, and some brands of pigment work better than others, but once you are happy with the pattern, seal it with a coat of matt varnish. That then leaves it open for the addition of transfers and weathering effects as you wish. I have been asked if a pattern was airbrushed and often get some surprised reactions when I say it was done with pigments.

Disruptive camouflage created by the use of pigments.

A second example of a pigment pattern.

Grey pigment for fading Panzer Grey.

I also like the effects of using a light grey pigment and rubbing it into the Panzer Grey surface of a model to provide some fading effect to the paint. The natural oils from your skin help it to adhere and blend into the paint itself.

MARKINGS

National Markings

In the early stages of World War II, with the invasion of Poland, German equipment carried a solid white cross as a national ID marking. However, experience in combat showed that against the dark grey paint used on German vehicles, these clear white crosses made for excellent aiming points for enemy anti-tank gunners. Some individual crews daubed the centre of the crosses with mud to try to reduce their clarity, while others used yellow paint to dull down the centre section of the cross. The next stage was to use just the four edges of the cross stencilled in white; these tended to vary in the thickness of the lines. It soon became a case of a black cross with the corners lined in white and that was used for much of the war, usually on the sides and rear of

an AFV. One other interesting element to the story is that the German army made good use of captured equipment, such as Sherman tanks in both North Africa and later North-West Europe, along with T-34s on the Eastern Front. These often carried additional crosses, or they were painted well over-size to try to prevent them being shot at by their own side if the vehicle outline was recognized. This offers an opportunity to model something a bit out of the ordinary.

Tactical Numbering

A distinctive feature on German AFVs during the war was the series of tactical numbering used on turrets or on the sides of turretless AFVs, often simply referred to as 'turret numbers'. Their colours varied, including plain white, plain black or plain red, or with the red or black numbers having white outlining, and, in a few cases, blue with white or yellow outlining. At the start of the war, the numbers were quite small, painted in white on a black rhomboid, either painted directly on to the vehicle, or on to small metal plates fitted to the vehicle.

The basic numbering system involved three numbers. The first represented the company, the

A T-34 in German colours and oversize national markings.

second the platoon and the third the individual vehicle within the platoon. If the second number was a 0, it represented one in the company head-quarters section. So, for a typical Panzer division, the numbers worked as follows:

- Company headquarters
    - 101 (company commander)
    - 102
- 1st platoon
    - 111 (platoon commander)
    - 112
    - 113
    - 114
- 2nd platoon
    - 121 (platoon commander)
    - 122
    - 123
    - 124

- 3rd platoon
    - 131 (platoon commander)
    - 132
    - 133
    - 134.

A common variation was used by regimental head-quarters units, where the first number was replaced with a capital letter R, so R01, R02. This occurred more so later in the war – for example, if the unit had more than nine companies, you could find a four-digit number. One of the best known examples was a Puma eight-rad armoured car captured in Normandy, which carried the turret number of 1111.

One disadvantage of this system was that the enemy could use that information, so some units did alter things to suit themselves. I make no attempt to even try to explain every variation that was used, but these are the basics.

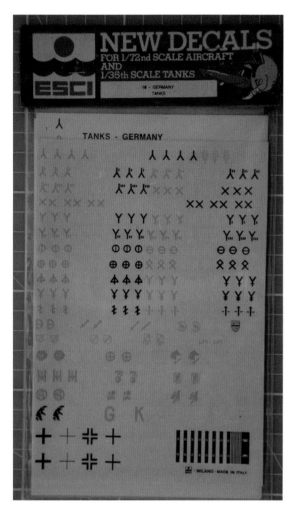

An old sheet of transfers from ESCI featuring divisional signs along with a few national and tactical markings.

Tactical Signs

German vehicles, armoured and soft-skins, used a series of tactical signs that denoted their user. This involved a series of shapes and designs used in combination to create the individual symbols. For example, a rhomboid shape represented a Panzer unit and a number alongside or within it identified the company. Other vehicle types would be identified by the addition of another element along the bottom of the shape, with two small circles to represent wheeled vehicles, or a single circle and an extended oval to represent a half-track. Just an extended oval by itself represented

a fully tracked vehicle. Other variations designated reconnaissance, signals, artillery units and many more. These symbols were all from an official guide that was amended in 1942, so the potential combinations, plus any local variations, make it far too big a topic even to attempt to include here. There are some very good descriptions, along with many illustrations of examples, within the book *Panzer Colours*, *Vol. 2* (*see* Bibliography). The symbols were generally applied by the use of stencils and were usually in white, although other colours were used occasionally.

Divisional/Unit Markings

At the outset of the war, the small divisional signs were often simple geometric shapes, but as the number of divisions was increased throughout the war, so more variations appeared. While such symbols had the potential to give away information to the enemy about the location of a particular unit, they were also important for the interests of morale in the parent unit, a pride in 'belonging' to a family. Some units did have shield designs that harked back to medieval shields and banners. There was a set of signs for the Wehrmacht, and others for the SS. For yet more variation, units such as the Herman Göring Panzer Division, as a Luftwaffe unit, had their own specialized designs. Then there were the Sturmgeschütz units, and still we have to add the Waffen-SS divisions.

There are plenty of good references among the Bibliography that can provide the details, rather than attempting to include them here. My particular favourite, as it includes reference photos, excellent artwork and background information, is *Panzer Colours*, *Vol. 2*.

Number Plates

These were used on almost all vehicles, though not the Panzers themselves. They consisted of black letters/numbers on a white background plate. The number was usually displayed on both front and back of the vehicle and preceded by two letters that indicated the service to which they belonged:

- WH = Wehrmacht Heere (Army)
- WL = Wehrmacht Luftwaffe (Air Force)
- WM = Wehrmacht Marine (Navy)
- SS = Waffen-SS
- POL = Polizei (Police)
- OT = Organisation Todt (this changed in 1944 to WT, when the Organisation was absorbed into the Wehrmacht).

Victory/Kill Markings

These were similar to how fighter pilots recorded their victories over enemy aircraft, with silhouettes or symbols to represent each one, so many gun crews liked to do the same thing. The most commonly seen were simple white bands around the gun barrel, each one representing a confirmed kill. Small silhouettes were also used either as an alternative, or sometimes a combination of both, representing a tank, armoured vehicle, truck or artillery piece.

TRANSFERS/DECALS

Kits by the major plastic manufacturers include waterslide transfers to add the various markings on the model, appropriate to the colour and marking choice you wish to build. The majority of resin and metal models, made by the so-called 'cottage industry' manufacturers, do not include transfers, so you will need to find your own. The first and cheapest solution is that when you build a plastic model there will most often be spare, unused transfers left over. Don't throw them away, but keep them to build-up your own collection of spares for when you might need them. As the years go, by this will become an ever more valuable resource. I will at this point add that when I was young these were always referred to as transfers. There has been an increasing tendency to refer to them as 'decals', but for our purposes they are essentially the same thing. My personal preference is still generally to refer to them as transfers.

There are two particular types of transfer. One is the more common waterslide transfer. You place these into (warm) water, so that the paper backing soaks through, allowing you to remove the piece from the water and literally slide the coloured transfer into place on your model. The individual design usually has an 'edge' of clear film, which in some cases needs to be trimmed off so that the transfer will fit up against an edge or part of the model. If a transfer needs trimming, do that before you put it into water. The trimming could be done with scissors or by scoring through the sheet with the sharp point of a craft knife. The fitting of the individual marking may need to conform to the shape of the model, which can be awkward. You can buy 'decal softener' to use instead of water, but I have found that the transfer can get so soft that it then shrinks up into an unusable mess. My preference therefore is to brush the softener liquid on to the model where the transfer is to fit. Slide the water-soaked transfer on to the model and adjust to get it into just the right place, then brush more of the softener on top. Use a cotton bud to press the transfer gently down and fix it in place. This technique also helps to prevent air bubbles getting caught underneath the transfer, causing an effect referred to as silvering.

The second type of transfer is 'dry rub'. These are generally thinner than the waterslide alternative. The design is held between two bits of paper, consisting of a backing sheet and a carrier sheet. As before, cut out the individual transfer that you want to use. Remove the backing sheet to expose the adhesive underside of the transfer. Carefully put it into place on the model exactly where you want it to go, as there is no leeway to adjust this type of transfer as you can a waterslide. Then, using a tool such as a ballpoint pen or the rounded end of a paintbrush handle, rub on top of the carrier sheet and it will release itself, leaving the thin transfer in place on the model. This technique can take a bit of practice to get right. Use a cotton bud again push the transfer gently into place. Dry-rub transfers don't have the silvering problem and generally look like they have been painted on.

There are sets of aftermarket transfers available for armour models, though they are not as extensive as the range available to aircraft modellers. For small-scale modellers, the ranges of both 15mm and 20mm scale sets available through the Plastic Soldier Company are perhaps the most extensive these days. There have also been some useful sets by Bison Decals (now Star Decals), which have some very neat sets for specific units/vehicles.

There has been a variety of transfer sheets available on the market over the years. The earliest I recall were those made by Almark in the 1970s. These have long been out of production, but you may still occasionally come across them at shows; I know Peter Bailey of Bull Models did have a few available. For larger scale models I would recommend the Star Decals range, along with others from Echelon Fine Detail, all waterslide transfers. The other one to mention, with a huge range of subjects in a mix of scales, is Archer Fine Transfers from the United States. The company also does waterslide and dry-rub ranges, both to a high quality.

SOME COLOUR REFERENCES

I feel it would be useful to round off this chapter with a few colour reference photos for the half-track fans. These are exterior and interior pictures of the genuine, restored SdKfz 250 Alte, the SdKfz 250 Neu and the basic SdKfz 251/1 Ausf D. With the 250 Alte in particular, you will see the later war Dunkelgelb and Dunkelgrun camouflage, but the interior remains in Panzer Grey. The other points about these are the details and colours of radios, and the crew kit stowed inside the vehicle, as well as the seats and internal fittings.

In these pictures you can see the answers to some of the questions that I have been asked most over the years, for example what the interior colour was for German half-tracks. The basic answer is that these open-top vehicles used the same colour inside and out, with the exception of those that were built prior to the significant changeover from Panzer Grey to the sand/green/red-brown of 1943. Units would repaint the external surfaces, but not the internal ones (engine compartment, troop compartment). Those built after 1943 would have had the Dunkelgelb painted at the factory as the base coat.

The other elements you can see in the pictures are the variety of internal stowage carried for the crew, along with radio equipment and instrument panels. Fortunately there are more

SdKfz 250 Alte – right side.

SdKfz 250 Alte – left side.

*SdKfz 250 Alte – open
engine compartment.*

instrument faces included on the transfer sheet of many modern kits, while companies such as Archer Fine Transfers in the USA also do a good selection for 1/35 models. You will notice that as well as the metal of the vehicle itself, there are other materials in use. The rifles, which are a mix of varnished wood and Gun Metal, also have leather carry straps. Note also, as seen here, that

LEFT: *SdKfz 250 Alte – dashboard and radio.*

BELOW: *SdKfz 250 Alte – rifle rack.*

the wooden stocks of the rifles varied in colour of wood, depending on where they were made and when. The mess tins are aluminium and show well-worn paint thanks to their daily use. Machine guns seen here have Gun Metal main bodies, but the handles were sometimes wood and sometimes a material such as Bakelite.

RIGHT: *SdKfz 250 Neu – left side.*

BELOW: *SdKfz 250 Neu – right side.*

To paint Gun Metal, I like to use black, then rub it with graphite powder to give a metallic sheen to the highlights. For leather straps, a number of paint manufacturers produce paint shades that match various shades of leather. Webbing pouches would be an appropriate matt colour, while ammunition pouches were black leather. The round gas-mask containers were metal,

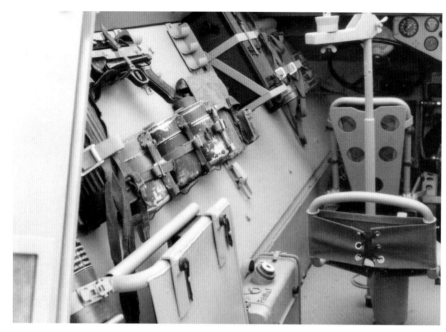

SdKfz 250 Neu – left-hand interior stowage.

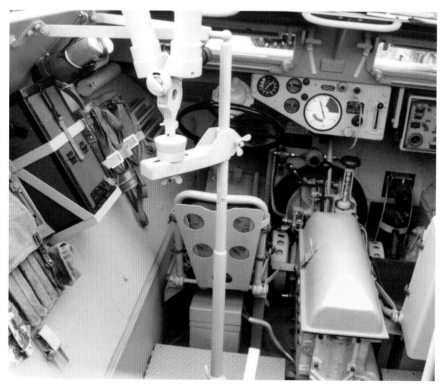

SdKfz 250 Neu – driver's position.

painted in Field Grey usually, but again would suffer from chips and knocks due to being carried around. In the case of the bench seats, these were wooden slats, so plain wood is another colour to be reproduced and weathered. There are all sorts of extra bits of information in this set of photos to help you get the colours right for all the additional stowage items.

SdKfz 250 Neu – right-side interior stowage.

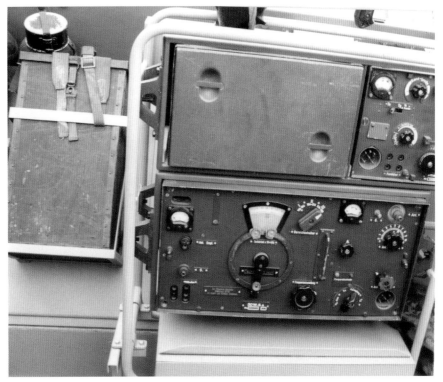

SdKfz 250 Neu – radio.

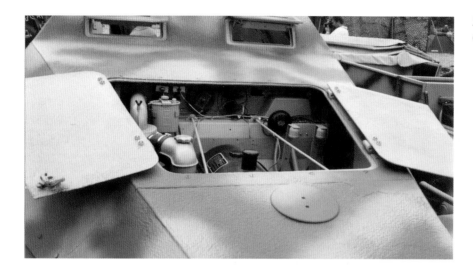

*SdKfz 251/1 Ausf D –
engine compartment.*

*SdKfz 251/1 Ausf D –
interior seating.*

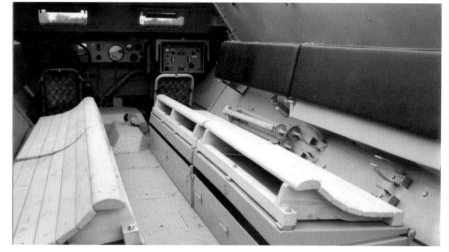

*SdKfz 251/1 Ausf D –
front MG42 mounting.*

THE PzKpfw VI Tiger I and Tiger II

After a couple of earlier unsuccessful designs, the Henschel-designed VK4501went into production as the Tiger I, perhaps the most famous of all wartime tanks. In many accounts, the attacking German tanks were referred to as 'Tigers', even when we know there were no Tiger-equipped units in the area. The impact of the fame of the tank, and indeed the fear of it, took over. The appearance of the Tiger I changed little during its production life, with the same basic hull and turret, which carried the powerful 8.8cm KwK36 L/56 main gun. It was notable for having inter-leaved road wheels that had rubber-rims, although these were later replaced with steel-wheeled alter-natives as the availability of rubber became ever more difficult. It also had two alternative sets of track. The widest track was used for combat, to spread out the weight of the tank and reduce the ground pressure, but when out of the line and to be prepared for rail transport, the outermost road wheels were removed, a narrower set of 'trans-port tracks' were fitted and the track guards on both sides of the hull were removed, which made it narrower overall, so that it could be carried on a standard-size railway flat car. Early versions carried some smaller stowage bins on the turret, fitted to either side, unlike the most commonly used single bin fitted to the back. Those early versions also had pipework and filters of the Feifel air-cleaner system, though this was susceptible to damage and this feature was removed.

Over 1,300 Tiger Is were produced between 1942 and August 1944 and they saw action on all fronts. The first examples were rushed into combat near Leningrad in August 1942 and others went to North Africa in 1943, where one was captured and returned to the UK for evaluation, now living on as Tiger 131 at the Tank Museum. Some Tigers also carried *zimmerit* paste on both the turret and hull, though not all.

One variant on the Tiger chassis was the 38cm Sturmmorser (Sturmtiger), The turret was removed and a tall fixed superstructure was added to carry the large 38cm weapon, which fired rocket-assisted ammunition used as a demolition vehicle to knock down fortifications/buildings. Only eight-een of these were made.

The Tiger II came about from the requirement to carry the larger and more powerful KwK43 L/71 main gun. The new hull design owed something to the smaller Panther, with well-sloped armour plate and 150mm thick frontal armour and 80cm on the sides. The longer hull had nine sets of inter-leaved road wheels. One visual factor was that the first fifty Tiger II hulls were fitted with a Porsche-designed turret that had a streamlined pattern, although with what proved to be something of a shot trap under the mantlet. A redesigned Henschel turret was used for the main production series, which led to a total of 489 Tiger IIs being built, including the 509 with the Porsche turret. The Tank Museum at Bovington is fortunate to have an example with each style of turret.

One other variant was built on the Tiger II chassis, the Jagdtiger, with a 12.8cm PaK 44 L/55 mounted in a fixed superstructure and a slightly lengthened hull. Only seventy-seven of these were built between 1944–5. Just two were made with an experimental Porsche suspension, which did not work, so the torsion-bar Henschel design from the standard gun tank was used instead. Interestingly, one of the rare Porsche suspension test vehicles is in the Tank Museum collection at Bovington.

Having mentioned the fifty Porsche turrets, these were built for a Porsche-designed tank that did not get a production order, but some turrets had been already made, as had a number of Porsche-designed hulls. The hulls were utilized by fitting a fixed superstructure and mounting the PaK 43 L/71, a heavily armoured tank hunter referred to as both the Ferdinand and the Elefant.

Chapter Seven

Taking the Next Steps – Adding Extra Detailing

There is lots of potential to add detailing to your AFV models. It may be adding more refined detail, battle damage and general wear and tear, correcting errors in a basic kit, as these do sometimes happen, or adding the additional stowage that crews carried on the outside due to lack of internal storage space within the vehicle.

For the modeller, where we are today regarding adding detail, stowage and placing models in dioramas owes a lot to the work of the Belgian modeller, François Verlinden. His work in modelling magazines and his huge range of resin kits and conversions, figures, stowage sets and diorama accessories, such as German bunkers,

A Verlinden Productions catalogue and a selection of their publications.

was an inspiration to many, including me, during the 1970s and 80s. His individual painting style created a distinctive look to his AFV models, which did generate some discussion, but whether one liked it or not, Verlinden can't be faulted for contributing a step change to the world of modelling (he made aircraft as well as AFVs and figures).

STOWAGE

Stowage can involve a wide variety of things. It can be minimal, maybe crew kit hung on the side of the turret, packs or bedrolls, or it might be racks of jerrycans with extra fuel and water, commonly used in North Africa and the vast expanses of the Russian Steppe. In theatres such as North-West Europe and Italy, it was more usually only one or two extra cans. Other spares could be carried, such as replacement road wheels or boxes of rations or smaller spares. Ammunition boxes could be among them, but not so often, as exposed to fire they would be too vulnerable most of the time. With tanks, rear decks would generally be left clear enough to allow the

turret to be rotated through the full 360 degrees without obstruction.

Some kits include stowage items, but not all. Fortunately, there are a number of aftermarket manufacturers who do packs of stowage items, or in some cases sets customized for specific models. In 1/35, in the USA Value Gear does a wide selection of very good value and there are others from the likes of Black Dog, Plus Models and Legend Productions. In small scale, there are also plenty of options, with a variety of sets from the likes of SHQ, Sgts Mess, MMS (all in white metal) and from Milicast in resin. German fuel drums and jerrycans are available for plastic kits. Tamiya did a pack many years ago that is still available and, more recently, Bronco Models has done one in 1/35 and others in both 1/48 and 1/72.

ETCHED DETAILING

Another level of detail which was once the domain of aftermarket producers only is that involving etched-brass detailing. Over recent years, however,

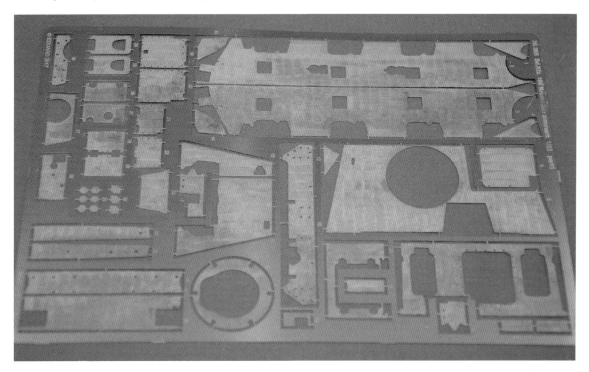

Eduard etched-metal zimmerit *panels to fit the Tamiya Brummbar.*

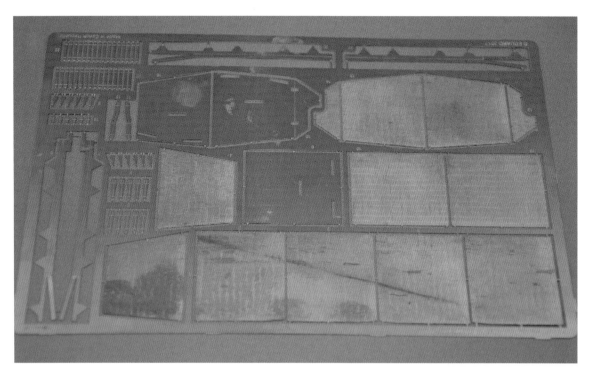

Another Eduard set, this time the zimmeri- coated side armour and supports for the Tamiya Brummbar.

more of the plastic kit manufacturers have begun to include some etched details within their base kits. Dragon Models, Trumpeter and Bronco Models all commonly include etched parts now. Even in small scale, Dragon includes some with a few of its 1/72 kits, as does Modelcollect.

Alternatively, there are some long-time producers of etched-brass detailing sets, two of which include Voyager and Eduard Models. The level of detail available with these can be amazing, though at times some of the small parts can be really fiddly to apply. Sometimes I might choose to use a complete set, but at other times leave off some of the tiniest detail. I did, for example, persevere with some etched tool brackets (for shovels and so on) which I found rather fiddly, but the end result did look good. Interesting that a number of kits these days include two sets of tools, one with moulded-on brackets and another without.

The one thing I would definitely suggest is to invest in one of the etched-brass bending tools, which are available in different sizes and are very useful in achieving nice, straight edges. One word about using etched brass is that it helps to 'anneal' the metal by holding it in a flame, using a candle or over a gas cooker if you have one. Clearly this needs to be done with great care and you need to hold the metal fret with something like a wooden clothes peg or long tweezers – it must be something that won't conduct the heat to your hand. This process helps to remove the 'springiness' of the metal, especially if you need to roll the part, not just make a sharply angled bend.

TURNED METAL GUN BARRELS

With plastic kits, the main gun barrels are most frequently moulded in two halves. Once these are joined together, there is almost always a join seam, which then needs to be removed. This can be done by the gentle use of a file or sanding paper, or even scraping it with a sharp craft knife. The danger is that the seam can remain visible, or that there will be a 'flat' spot on the cylindrical barrel. There are a number of models on the market these days where new 'slide moulding' techniques allow the barrels to be made in one piece, while other kits include turned aluminium or brass barrels.

Most barrels still come in two plastic halves, however. So, if you want to replace one with a turned metal barrel there are a number of manufacturers who make them. The first I remember on the market came from Jordi Rubio in Spain, though more recently RB Models in Poland does a wide range of barrels in different scales. It is well worth checking out the company's website (http://www.rbmodel.com/).

ZIMMERIT

Zimmerit was a factory-applied concrete-like anti-magnetic mine paste applied to the surfaces of German AFVs from the end of 1943 to the end of 1944. Apparently its use was stopped because there was a risk that it could catch fire, though it

never did. Cutting it did speed up the production process, however. It was mainly used on tanks and various Jagdpanzer. Perhaps its most interesting use was on the Ferdinand/Elefant, where it was stopped halfway up the superstructure, on the basis that it was not possible to reach up higher to affix the mine.

A variety of patterns was used, mostly down to which factory the tank had come from. When I began modelling, the only way to add the *zimmerit* pattern was to place a coat of very thin filler over the model, then engrave the chosen pattern by hand. There have been tools available over the years that helped to create the patterns. Another alternative was to use a pyrogravure, a heated engraving tool, to engrave the pattern directly into the plastic of the kit. However, in recent years there have been etched sheets of *zimmerit*, pre-shaped for particular subjects, along with some others doing the same thing, but made with a

Zimmerit *on a real vehicle, the Henschel-turreted King Tiger at Bovington.*

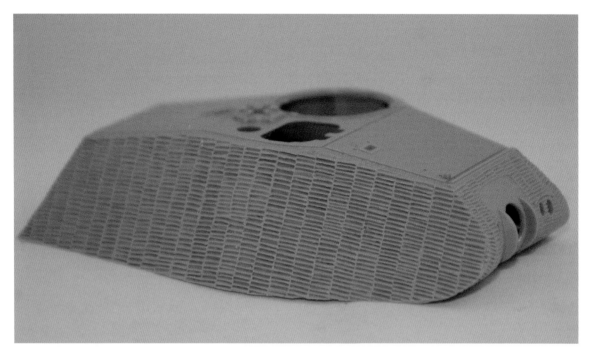

Dragon has made a nice job of moulding the pattern seen here on the Porsche turret for the King Tiger.

For small-scale fans, these Panthers are made by The Plastic Soldier Company.

This zimmerit *pattern is seen on the Panzer IV at the Musée des Blindes at Saumur, France.*

Another pattern from Saumur, this time on the Sturmpanzer Brummbar.

Yet another different style, this time on the Saumur Jagdpanther.

thin and flexible resin casting. More recently still, kit manufacturers have been able to mould kits reliably with the *zimmerit* pattern already on the kit. Dragon, in particular, has done some very nice kits with this moulded-on coating. In small scale, the Plastic Soldier Company has done Panther and Tiger I kits that have a *zimmerit* pattern.

INTERIOR DETAILING

Most AFV kits do not have interior detail, part of the reason being that most models are built 'closed up' so the detail can't be seen in the finished model anyway. You can section a model, which would enable you to see some of it. Some models have partial internal detail, so they may contain the engine compartment, while others just have detail in the crew compartment. Interior detailing also means a lot more parts and hence a lot more work in completing the build. That, in turn, will also be

likely to increase the cost of the kit. I've been interested to see that Takom has started to do different versions of its King Tiger kits, either with or without the interior detail. The same is also being done for the Panther kits.

Open-top AFVs usually include internal details of their open crew compartment. Going back many years, a Japanese manufacturer, Bandai, produced a series of 1/48 scale models which did include some basic internal details for both engine and crew compartments. They were good kits for their day, but somehow 1/48 armour did not gain enough popularity and the range ceased production. These days, you can find some of them for sale online or from an online second-hand kit seller. I remember seeing a couple of stacks of them on a trader's table at an AMPS show in Atlanta, Georgia. A couple of hours later when I went past again, all had gone, proving them to be quite collectable now.

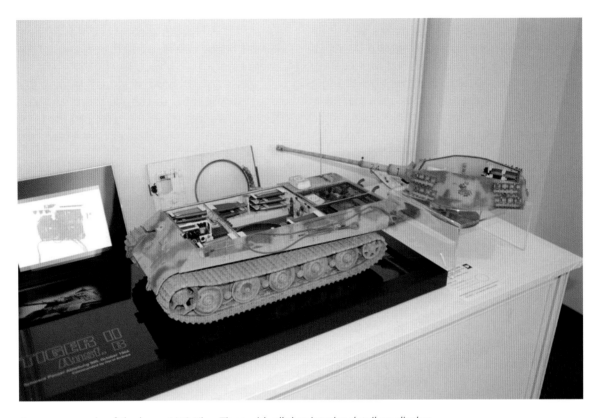

A super example of the huge 1/16 King Tiger with all that interior detail on display,
seen at EuroMilitaire back in 2012.

At about the same time, another Japanese model manufacturer, Nitto, also produced a series of 1/76 models that included some basic internal details (engine, turret basket, driver seat and so on). Some of those models were good, one or two maybe not quite so good, but Nitto stopped adding more to the range and was acquired by Fujimi, which continues to hold the kits on its list.

Most recently, there has been a huge 1/16 King Tiger from Trumpeter that has all the interior detail, but this is far from a 'pocket-money' kit. Such a large model will certainly make an impressive display piece, but how many of these super-size models can you keep in your house? Smaller in scale, one of the new manufacturers, Modelcollect, has recently done a Special Edition of its E75, a Paper Panzer design, which includes full interior detail, including the crew figures to fit in their positions, etched detail

parts and mesh grilles, plus a load of super etched-brass circular bases for all the ammunition rounds in their racks.

DIORAMAS
A diorama consists of the careful positioning of a number of objects in a realistic setting. Many museums create diorama displays in full size, while modellers can build them in any chosen scale. Whether or not you build your models in dioramas will be a question of personal preference. I have to admit that personally I don't generally build dioramas because I simply don't have enough space to keep them. What I do have are two or three scenic bases on which I can put different vehicles for photographic purposes.

The inspiration for many dioramas comes from archive photos, which you can recreate in model form, although others may simply come from the modeller's imagination. There are plenty of examples of dioramas to be found in modelling magazines if you would like to see how they get put together, while model shows are a great way to see the vast range of possibilities that can be achieved. In addition to the vehicles, there can be groundwork, water, vegetation, buildings to recreate, as well as seasonal times of year, from the heat of the desert to the deep snows of the Eastern Front.

If you want to build dioramas there are a number of elements to consider once you have decided on a scene you want to recreate, so to do this let's look at some examples I have seen over the years at various events.

An overall view of the huge Clervaux diorama.

The most impressive diorama I have seen is 'Diorama Clervaux' by Claude Joachim, who has even produced a book about it. He has shown the scene with US troops back in control, but it was a (real) hotel and village involved in the fighting during the Ardennes Offensive of December 1944, the Battle of the Bulge. He started with the hotel itself, but has gradually added more sections so now it is not only superbly built and detailed, but HUGE! He brought part of it to EuroMilitaire back in 2007 when the hotel itself was on display, but he returned again in 2010 with the whole thing and it was the great attraction in the foyer at the event. A diorama like this would take years of planning and dedication to bring to completion and Joachim is clearly a master of his art.

Detail from the Clervaux diorama, showing how well the different surfaces such as stone, wood and plaster have been done.

ABOVE: *More detail from the Clervaux diorama. War-damaged roof, but civilian life has to carry on amidst everything else.*

LEFT: *Staying with the Clervaux diorama, as well as showing the size of this project, detail even at the back and the ivy/ vegetation on the turret look ideal.*

A final indication of the detail from the Clervaux diorama, showing figures, furniture and the even the internal roof joists.

An entry at EuroMilitaire in 2005, showing vehicles and figures in a maintenance scene

Some detail of the maintenance work being undertaken on the Panther, plus appropriate figures and little bits of detail laying around.

Using another example, maintenance/recovery scenes are popular. Here is one seen at EuroMilitaire back in 2005. It is a large diorama and will have involved a lot of work. In addition to the work involved in building the main vehicle, the modeller has also done figures, groundwork and buildings. A scene such as this will have involved a long period of construction. The end result makes for an excellent scene, but not many of us will be lucky enough to have the space to store many dioramas as big as this. Other options are to sell it, or to donate it to a museum. I have spoken to some modellers who will even dismantle such a large piece.

Others dioramas can be a little smaller but manage to convey a sense of the region and season that they depict. It may be the dry terrain and dust of North Africa, or maybe the wet mud and snow of the Eastern Front.

A couple of smaller dioramas feature a single abandoned vehicle. In one case, we see an abandoned Flakpanzer 38(t), ditched in the Normandy countryside, taped off to indicate that it has yet to be checked by an EOD (Explosive Ordnance Disposal) team, but even though it is small, it causes a passing US paratrooper to stop and have a look at it.

The other diorama, representing a period perhaps in 1945 or maybe early 1946, shows chil-

'Thirsty Fox' is a desert scene, with the crew gathered around the dusty tank, creating a very dry and different atmosphere.

Another change of scene, with a Tiger I in the winter landscape of the Eastern Front, with a thatched building common to the Russian countryside. A good mix of snow and mud.

Another change of setting with this one, taped off and being looked at by a US paratrooper, a 2cm Flakpanzer based on the Pz 38(t) chassis in the Normandy bocage of 1944.

Quite a common sight at the end of the war, when the fighting has moved on. The abandoned Jagdtiger has been pushed aside, tracks gone. While the US trooper paints a US claim on the vehicle, it has become a natural climbing frame for the local children.

dren playing on an abandoned Jagdtiger while US troops mark it up with whitewash, indicating that it is ready for removal from the battlefield.

SCRATCH-BUILDING

It is many years since I scratch-built anything, largely due to the sheer volume of models that are now readily available on the market, so the number of modellers who take on a scratch-build project are getting ever fewer. Back in the 1960s, when I started modelling, to scratch-build some subjects was pretty much your only choice. The basic material was plastic card, which was and still is available in a variety of thicknesses. You also needed a set of scale drawings of your chosen subject to work from for measurements and angles. You also had to be sure that the drawings were accurate. When

cutting parts and choosing how to join them, it is equally important to consider, and allow for, the thickness of the card.

Scratch-building really remains in the hands of the more experienced modellers and therefore is not really within the scope to be included here in more detail. I still have a Ferdinand/Elefant which I scratch-built over forty years ago, using road wheels from the old Airfix Tiger I kit and cut-down track from the same source. It isn't brilliant, but it did mean that I had an example in my collection before a kit was available on the market and it is still recognizable as an Elefant.

The other option is a 'conversion', where you use an existing kit and convert it into a different variant. I can refer back to the 1960s when the only kits available were the Airfix range of the StuG III and the Panther. I converted the StuG by

Not a brilliantly made model, but one that has managed to survive for over forty years.

The Panther, a series of scale plans for all the production variants, is just one example from a series of books by Polish publisher Kagero.

Just a small selection of the 1/76 scale drawings by Geoff Lacey.

using the chassis of the StuG III, added the new superstructure and scratch-built the turret. In the same way, I used the Airfix Pz IV to create my first Jagdpanzer IV and then its Panther hull to convert it to a Jagdpanther. These days, pretty much everything is now available as a kit in one form or another and I really can't think of anything I would want that isn't available from somewhere.

However, if you still want to scratch-build a model there are scale drawings available from a variety of sources. For a host of reasons they can be slightly out, so it is best to double-check measurements if you can. Luckily these days, once you have a set you are happy with and in whatever scale, modern photocopiers and computers allow you to scale them up or down as you need. One of my long-time friends, Geoff Lacey, has created hundreds of sets of drawings over the years, covering all sorts of nationalities that include German equipment, although as Geoff is not an Internet user, these are not available online.

THE LIGHT HALF-TRACK SERIES

Based on a slightly shortened chassis of the SdKfz 10, a light half-track troop carrier, an armoured version, the 250, was required for reconnaissance units. There were two main variations. The original one is referred to as the 'Alte' (old), of which over 4,000 were built between 1941–3. In the interests of simplifying the design for production, the 'Neu' (new) version was produced between 1944–5 (another 2,300). A good indication of why the changes were made is that the Alte version involved nineteen plates of armour, while the Neu version used just nine. This factor alone clearly made great savings in manufacturing time and labour.

There were twelve official subvariants on the 250 chassis, built for specialized purposes. These included:

- SdKfz 250/1 – the basic troop carrier version that was built throughout the production life of the Alte and Neu versions, armed with 2 × MG34/42 and a two-man crew and carrying the half-platoon of troops (Halbgruppe)
- SdKfz 250/2 – crew of four and only 1 × MG34/42, cable laying for communications networks (telephone)
- SdKfz 250/3 – radio-equipped Command vehicle, with variations of radio carried depending upon user formation; used by both Wehrmacht and Luftwaffe ground units
- SdKfz 250/4 – was to be a light AA vehicle fitted with the Zwillingslafette dual MG34 mount, but this did not go into production and the designation was used for an observation vehicle (Panzer Beobachtungswagen)

- SdKfz 250/5 – another light observation variant, early versions with a frame antenna, and referred to as an Aufklärungspanzerwagen to differentiate it from the 250/4
- SdKfz 250/6 – an ammunition carrier, or Munitionspanzerwagen, commonly used with Sturmgeschütz units
- SdKfz 250/7 – Schützenpanzerwagen Granatwerfer, carried the 8cm mortar GrW34
- SdKfz 250/8 – mounted the 7.5cm KwK 37 L/24 for infantry support
- SdKfz 250/9 – carried a turret-mounted 2cm KwK 38, using the turret from the SdKfz 222 armoured car, which it replaced, and later the Hängelafette turret
- SdKfz 250/10 – mounted the 3.7cm PaK 35/36, with varying gunshields
- SdKfz 250/11 – an alternative to the 250/10, this variant carried the 2.8cm sPzB41, the squeeze gun anti-tank weapon designed for airborne troops
- SdKfz 250/12 – Messtruppenpanzerwagen, a survey and range-plotting vehicle issued to artillery units.

A number of other variations existed, though were not given an official designation, such as a Neu example fitted with a 5cm PaK 38.

One other variation, designated as the SdKfz 252, had a cut-down rear plate, commonly towed a small ammunition trailer and was an ammunition carrier for StuG units.

Chapter Eight
References – The Real Things

One of the things about modelling is that apart from the enjoyment/relaxation of the hobby itself, it can have some knock-on effects. I found myself falling victim to one of these effects over the years and thoroughly enjoying the consequences. As you make the models, going through the assembly tasks, identifying the parts on the sprues and in the instructions, you turn the parts over in your hands multiple times and your vehicle recognition skills improve exponentially. As your interest in the real thing grows, you want to find out more about them, perhaps what it would feel like to be inside them. The only thing you need to be careful of is something I have fallen foul of, in that if you watch a movie or TV programme, you will identify the 'wrong' vehicles used in films. You can rely on your family to let you know when they will no longer watch a film with you because they know you'll find fault in the tanks that have been used! One example is *The Battle of the Bulge*, in which the makers used formations of M47 Patton tanks to represent the German Panzers, or any number of films where US M3 half-tracks are supposed to be German. More recently, some film-makers have made much more effort to get it right. Some of the conversions done for *Saving Private Ryan* and *Band of Brothers* are difficult to recognize from the real thing even at quite close range.

As your hobby progresses, you will most likely find that you become an avid hunter of research information. Having said that, beware the potential for getting drawn into the point where the search for accurate detail and information stops you actually building your model. I wonder how many modellers, and this includes me, have begun building something and it then sits part-finished because they feel they need just that one more bit of information before committing to finishing the model? That result in a whole number of so-called 'shelf queens', which get put to one side, often boxed, and left there as other new projects grab your attention. It's a common problem.

ARCHIVE PHOTOS

There are thousands of books available today that present archive photos from World War II and this number grew immensely after the collapse of the Warsaw Pact and the end of the Cold War. Access to resources from Russia and Eastern Europe has opened up thousands of new images. After years of books that frequently repeated the same photos over and over, these days we see many collections of new images being published. The difficulty will be choosing which ones to buy, as it becomes impossible to get them all. Many can also be found thanks to the availability of the Internet.

MILITARY VEHICLE SHOWS

There are a good number of military vehicle rallies around the UK each year and these can hold all sorts of welcome surprises. The biggest of them all has to be the War and Peace Revival show in Kent. When it started it was a relatively small event, but it has grown to be what I believe is the largest such event in the world. I have known there to be over 4,000 vehicles on display over many acres in

A genuine StuG III Ausf D, one of just three used and captured in North Africa during the war and pictured soon after restoration was completed.

an event that lasts almost a week. Each year, you wonder just what you might find on show. You may find yourself walking past lines of Jeeps, Land Rovers, GMC trucks and so on, but then you can walk round a corner and find something special. Over the years, I can recall things like StuG IIIs, both real ones like the desertized Ausf D in 2016, and the replicas built for film and TV. Those created for *Saving Private Ryan* and *Band of Brothers* were built on the chassis of the British Army FV432 APC and are difficult to tell apart from a real one until you get close and see the road wheels. I have also seen a Jagdpanzer IV, a Panther, a Pz IV and other real StuG IIIs.

Another excellent event for the German AFV enthusiast has to be the annual Tankfest event at the Tank Museum, Bovington. Star of the events over the years has been Tiger 131, a Tiger tank captured in North Africa during World War II and returned to the UK for evaluation. It was restored to running condition in 2004 and has been a regular runner in the Tank Museum arena since then, drawing in thousands of visitors keen to see and hear an operating example of what is perhaps the most famous tank of all. The museum also now holds the full-size replica of the World War I A7V, which is also seen in the arena, though very slow moving, just like the original. Other exhibits

LEFT: *Tiger 131 is always star of the show when it drives into the arena at Tank Museum events such as Tiger Day or Tankfest.*

BELOW: *This restored StuG III was one of the visitors at Tankfest 2017.*

ABOVE: *Another visitor in 2017, the large Jagdpanther, also kept in running condition.*

RIGHT: *A visitor to Tankfest in 2016, in the Panzer Grey colours of the Blitzkrieg era, a Pz 38(t).*

displayed include the Panzer III and the museum also hosts visiting tanks, such as a StuG III and a Jagdpanther, which were at the 2017 event.

MUSEUM EXHIBITS

Museums are of course holders of examples of the real thing. Visiting them can let you find some real gems which are so worth seeing. Let me take you through a few that I have managed to visit over the years, though there are still many others that I would like to visit.

THE TANK MUSEUM, BOVINGTON

I have already mentioned the external annual event at Bovington, Tankfest, but there is much more to be seen there which remains non-operational

and makes up the static displays within the main museum buildings. One of the museum's newest displays is the Tiger Collection. In addition to Tiger 131, there are two examples of the Tiger II, or King Tiger. I believe it to be a unique display, as both the production Henschel turret and the rare Porsche turret are shown side by side. The Porsche-designed turret had been built for an alternative design that was not ordered, though fifty turrets had been built, so these were used on the Henschel-designed chassis.

Another part of the exhibit is the even bigger Jagdtiger, armed with the 12.8cm gun. This is a particularly rare example, as it is one of just two built with a Porsche suspension system, unlike the main production versions, which used the same interleaved road wheels as used on the King Tigers. To round off the Tiger collection is a vehicle brought

Panzerjäger Ferdinand on show at Bovington.

over on loan from the USA and the only example to be found here in the UK, the Panzerjäger Ferdinand. This has a large fixed superstructure on the chassis designed by Ferdinand Porsche that was his unsuccessful submission for the contract for the Tiger I, the chassis that would have had the classic Tiger I turret fitted to it. Only two of those were built as gun tanks and in recent years photos have emerged that they were actually issued to a combat unit, schwerer Panzerjäger Abteilung 653, which used them as Command vehicles for their Ferdinand tank destroyers.

There are, of course, other German armour exhibits at the Tank Museum and its Pz III Ausf L is another regular in the events arena, while static displays in the museum include Pz III and IV, the small Pz I Ausf B Kleiner Panzerbefehlswagen, the light armoured Command vehicle. As well as a

couple of StuG IIIs, there is also an SdKfz 251 Ausf C, which is different for being the earlier pattern example and not the simplified bodywork of the later Ausf D versions. The Tank Museum is one of the best armour museums in the world and well worth a visit and stands out for its annual Tankfest event, when you get the chance to see so many of the collection being run in arena displays – the opportunity to both hear and see them on the move is a rare privilege.

THE IMPERIAL WAR MUSEUM, DUXFORD

The Imperial War Museum site at Duxford in Cambridgeshire is well worth visiting. Though the number of German AFVs to be found there is limited, it does have a fine selection of German artil-

A preserved StuG III on display at the IWM Duxford, Cambridgeshire.

lery on display. The museum's one special vehicle, which was once kept there, was a rare Heuschreke ('Grasshopper'), though I understand it was sold to a collection in the USA a few years ago.

MUSÉE DES BLINDÉS, SAUMUR, FRANCE

Perhaps the best collection of WW2 German AFVs can be found at the French tank museum,

the Musée des Blindés at Saumur. Sadly, the museum does not have a display arena in the way that Bovington does, so its 'runners' may be seen in parades in the town, or at some events during the year they can be run within the confines of the car park. What is inside the museum halls, though, is a marvellous selection, thanks largely to the numbers captured intact from the Normandy campaign of 1944.

Saumur's Tiger I is in good external condition and is particularly interesting for being displayed with the narrower transport tracks.

The heavier tanks of the second half of the war needed equally capable recovery versions, evident here from the size of this Bergepanther.

Jagdpanzer IV L/70A.

Marder IIIM, the later version based on the modified chassis of the Pz 38(t), with the engine moved forward and a 7.5cm Pak 40 mounted in a lightly armoured superstructure.

Another variation on the Marder III at Saumur, this time the Russian 7.62cm gun with a simple shield fitted to the hull of a Pz 38(t).

In the grey colour of the early war, a Pz II that is also in working order. Of particular interest is that the aerial trough is/was made of wood, not metal.

A late-war Pz IV, complete with the camouflage scheme of dark yellow, green, red-brown, zimmerit paste and mesh side skirts.

15cm Panzerwerfer 42, a self-propelled half-track mounting the 15cm Nebelwerfer launch tubes.

Inside the 15cm Panzerwerfer 42 body the storage racks can be seen for the spare rockets ready to reload. Italeri does a neat kit of this.

Bastogne Barracks, Belgium

Part of the Belgian Army Museum, the collection at Bastogne Barracks in southern Belgium is well worth a visit. It is free to enter, but you have to go on guided tours at specific times of the day rather than just wander round at your leisure. There are lots of interesting vehicles and displays to be found here, not all German, and a trip into the work-

RIGHT: *The dismantled StuG III allowed for a close-up view of many detail fittings.*

BELOW: *Nearing completion, with engine and fighting compartment reinstalled, but before the roof was refitted to the fighting compartment.*

shops I found fascinating. On my first visit they had taken apart a StuG II Ausf F8 ready for restoration and when I went back a year later a very different looking StuG was nearing completion. I understand it is now complete and on display in the vehicle hanger.

LEFT: *Still in original colours, a German conversion on a captured French UE carrier used for patrol duties by occupation forces/Luftwaffe airfield defence.*

BELOW: *A Panzer IV in the collection at Bastogne Barracks.*

NACHF collection, Fort Benning, Georgia

It was back in 2013 when I had the opportunity to fulfil one of my long-term wishes. Until that point I had never been to the USA, but had long wanted to see the armour collections at both Fort Knox and at the Aberdeen Proving Grounds, Maryland. Both of those collections closed before I could get to see them, but fortunately the Fort Knox collection was moved to Fort Benning, along with a large number of the exhibits from Aberdeen. So, I was lucky that in one visit I could see both in one go, now in the hands of the National Armour Cavalry Heritage Foundation (NACHF). One unique exhibit

is the only example of the Panther II, though the hull never had the intended new turret fitted, so it has an Ausf G turret instead.

Alongside it in the hanger is a well-restored King Tiger, a Henschel-turreted version. It has sections of armour removed on the left-hand side of both hull and turret, so you can clearly see the interior arrangements. This was done to create a training aid when it was used at a Training School for tank crews in the US.

Among other German AFVs at Fort Benning are a number of others that have their own interesting features. There is a StuG III that remains in the original camouflage colours from World War II, as

The one surviving Panther II hull at Fort Benning in 2013.

Sectioned King Tiger at Fort Benning, seen here in 2013.

This StuG III is one which has managed to survive still with its original camouflage colours.

it has escaped any effort to repaint it since then. The vehicle remains in good external condition, kept inside, so while the colours have faded over the seventy years since the war, they are a marvellous reference.

Close by in the hanger is a Panzer IIF, a Pz III and one I particularly liked, a restored SdKfz 251/9 Ausf D. Outside are a number of Panthers, which are awaiting more restoration, along with a Jagdtiger and an SdKfz 234 with 75mm Pak 40. You will even find pallets with spare tracks.

RIGHT: *Pz II Ausf F.*

BELOW: *A genuine SdKfz 251/9 with short 75mm gun.*

THE BATTLEFIELDS

As well as museums, a trip to the battlefields is well worth it if you want to get an even better impression of the 'feel' of sites where the events of World War II took place. The Continent is easy enough to get to by car these days, thanks to the various ferry routes, while my personal preference is the Channel Tunnel, which helps make day trips to the Pas de Calais region a very realistic thing to do, while if you have longer, say a week or two, then I can't recommend highly enough a trip to Normandy. You can find a good number of museums in the area that have plenty of exhibits of both German and Allied equipment. There are, of course, a host of bunkers and defence works worth seeing as well. For me, though, there are sites you can still clearly identify from archive photos, and to visit them gives a greater sense of the atmosphere of an area. One of these sites, or more strictly three, revolves around one of the most famous German tank commanders of the war, Michael Wittman.

The first is to visit Villers-Bocage, where, on 13 June 1944, units of the 22nd Armoured Brigade, part of 7th Armoured Division, were effectively ambushed by Tiger I tanks of the 101st SS Heavy Panzer Battalion under the command of Michael Wittmann. There are plenty of archive photos that illustrate the results of the battle, when Wittman and his unit advanced down the road into the village, knocking out a while series of British armoured vehicles as they went. Even though the town had to be largely rebuilt after the war, you can still recognize certain points along the road. An excellent photo-record of the battle by my friend Dan Taylor, *Villers-Bocage Through the Lens*, has a fine collection of the photos which illustrate the course of the fight.

Later, on 8 August, Wittman's tank, tactical number 007, was knocked out near the village of Saint-Aignan-de-Cramesnil. His was one of three Tigers knocked out in a field, to shots accredited to Trooper Joe Ekins, the gunner of a Sherman Firefly. Wittman's tank was stopped near the side of a main road, which is now a quiet place that is easy to park by, as a modern dual carriageway has taken the traffic away from the spot. If you drive across a nearby lane that leads across the fields into Saint-Aignan-de-Cramesnil you get to a line of trees, where Joe Ekins' Firefly was situated, and there is a memorial with flags and a mounted picture that indicates the positions of the units and individual AFVs on that fateful day. When I visited the site, by chance I met the mayor of the village, and this was just a few months after I had the privilege of meeting Joe Ekins himself during the Tankfest event at the Tank Museum, Bovington, prior to his death in 2012.

The third and final element of a visit is to the German Cemetery at La Cambe. Wittmann and his crew were buried in an unmarked roadside grave, where they were discovered in 1983 and moved to a permanent site at La Cambe.

While still in Normandy, a bit further south from the beaches, look out for the Tiger in Vimoutiers. Thought to have been on the strength of schwere Panzer Abteilung 503 in August 1944, this Tiger was one of several on their way to a fuel dump when leaving the Falaise Pocket. However, it ran out of fuel before it got there and was abandoned by its crew on the road from Lisieux to Alençon (the Route Nationale 179), just outside Vimoutiers. The crew made an attempt to set demolition charges, which buckled the engine deck and jammed the turret, leaving it in the middle of the road.

It was later bulldozed into the roadside by US troops, where it remained for the next thirty years. It was sold after the war to a scrap merchant, who did little more than remove the gearbox and left it to rust away by the roadside. When the scrap company owner died, it was sold to another, yet when they started to try to remove it, the townspeople of Vimoutiers protested and in the end the Tiger was purchased by the town. It came to prominence thanks to the story being featured in *After the Battle* magazine in 1975 and the Tiger was recovered to find a permanent home, supported on a concrete plinth, at the side of the road very near to where it was actually abandoned by its crew all those years ago.

The Vimoutiers Tiger, with the wider combat track and later steel road wheels.

There is a lay-by and parking alongside, so it is easy to stop for a picnic, or just to look at the Tiger. The Tiger has late steel road wheels and the smaller style of muzzle brake on the 88mm gun. Some parts were removed by the scrap merchants, such as the hatches, part of the engine deck, external exhaust parts and all the smaller fittings. The damage from the demolition charges, where the armour has been split from internal explosion(s), is still there for all to see. It is a very interesting roadside memorial, being very much an 'original' to the site. I took a set of photos in 2008, having detoured from the Autoroute on our way home from Saumur especially to see it.

There remain many places, museums and memorials I would like to see. If I have one regret, it is that I left it until I was fifty before I started travelling on the Continent, so I would encourage you to start earlier than that if you can. There is just so much to see.

THE CEMETERIES

One element of visiting the battlefields which I personally consider a 'must' is to visit the variety of War Cemeteries that you find almost anywhere you go. I have already mentioned the German Cemetery at La Cambe, which is on the major road between Caen and Bayeux, the N13. It is maintained by the German War Graves Commission (Volksbund Deutsche Kriegsgräberfürsorge) and contains over 21,000 graves. The main American Cemetery is at Colleville-sur-Mer, overlooking Omaha Beach, while numerous British and Commonwealth War Grave Cemeteries can be found throughout the Normandy area, as well as the rest of Western Europe, all so well maintained by the Commonwealth War Graves Commission (CWGC). As with Michael Wittman and his crew, you will find headstones in many of the CWGC sites that are placed butted up against each other, not spaced as they usually are, with the names of tank crew who were obviously recovered together from a single vehicle. It indicates that the individual bodies could not be clearly identified so they are buried together. A similar arrangement is often seen with aircraft crews.

I include this information as it is worth remembering those troops of all sides who died during the war. I always find these sites moving places to visit, but make a point of stopping at those I come across while driving. The only thing I would warn you of, especially in the CWGC cemeteries, is that the relatives' comments in the visitors' books always reduce me to tears. Any visit is worthwhile as an act of remembrance for so many and a reminder of the realities of a subject that has occupied our hobby time, in my case for over fifty years.

Based on the chassis of the unarmoured SdKfz 11 half-track, when fitted with an angular armoured body the SdKfz became a widely used armoured vehicle that went through some variants of Ausf A, B, C and D, each of which introduced particular changes that can be recognized. These were also used for about twenty-three different specialized roles, some of which were done using either Ausf C or Ausf D variants. The Ausf A was very similar in layout to the Ausf B, but had vision ports on the sides of the body for the use of the troops it carried, but these were deleted from all subsequent versions. The Ausf D retained the same basic body shape, though the shape of the front end was changed, with a larger front plate and extensions to the air intakes on the sides of the engine compartment. More simplifications came with the Ausf D, again to the front plate, and the removal of those little bulges on the engine compartment, and, most obvious, simplifications to the rear body, changing the arrangement of the stowage boxes on the track guards and blending them into the hull sides. The rear door was also simplified into a flatter shape, rather than the angled shape of the earlier marks. Following is a list of the different types:

- SdKfz 251/1 – the SPW (Schützenpanzerwagen) was the basic APC, though the designation was also used for a version fitted with large side frames to launch six of the larger Werfer rounds (28cm high explosive and/or 32cm Incendiary)
- SdKfz 251/2 – equipped with the 8cm Granatwerfer ('grenade thrower')
- SdKfz 251/3 – radio-equipped Command version, a Funkpanzerwagen, which could carry a variety of radio set-ups depending on specific role
- SdKfz 251/4 – ammunition carrier, commonly used alongside the SdKfz 251/9
- SdKfz 251/5 – Radio Command vehicle for Engineer units, but a short lived version
- SdKfz 251/6 – Command Post
- SdKfz 251/7 – a Pioneerpanzerwagen, an Engineer's variant, especially recognizable by the small assault bridges on racks on the sides of the hull
- SdKfz 251/8 – Krankenpanzerwagen, an armoured ambulance designed to carry two stretcher cases or four sitting wounded
- SdKfz 251/9 – known as the 'Stummel', this carried a 7.5cm gun to provide infantry support firepower; two styles of mounting were used, the change simply to make production easier
- SdKfz 251/10 – issued to troop leaders, this mounted the 3.7cm PaK 35/36 above the driver's cab in place of the front MG mounting
- SdKfz 251/11 – Fernsprechpanzerwagen, a telephone exchange and cable layer
- SdKfz 251/12 – Messtrupp und Geratpanzerwagen, a radio-equipped artillery survey vehicle
- SdKfz 251/13 – Schallaufnahmepanzerwagen, equipped with artillery sound recording equipment
- SdKfz 251/14 – Schallauswertepanzerwagen, an artillery sound ranging vehicle
- SdKfz 251/15 – Lichtauswertepanzerwagen, an artillery flash spotter
- SdKfz 251/16 – Flammpanzerwagen, fitted with two flame projectors mounted on each side of the superstructure
- SdKfz 251/17 – Schützenpanzerwagen, in varying formats, an SP mounting for the 2cm AA gun, with re-shaped side panels that could be folded down or with a pedestal mounted gun with small shield
- SdKfz 251/18 – Beobachungspanzerwagen, a radio equipped observation vehicle
- SdKfz 251/19 – Fernsprechbetriebspanzerwagen, a mobile telephone exchange
- SdKfz 251/20 – Infrarotscheinwerfer, a large infra-red light projector which was intended to work alongside infra-red light-equipped Panther units
- SdKfz 251/21 – mounted a three-gun unit of the MG151/15 AA 'Drilling'
- SdKfz 251/22 – mounted a 7.5cm PaK 40, with the carriage removed and a cut-out in the cab roof to allow for gun traverse
- SdKfz 251/23 – fitted with a 20mm gun in the Hängelafette turret, also used on the SdKfz 234/1 eight-rad armoured car.

Added to these were various field conversions and experimental types which never received an official designation, but can be seen in archive photos. One of the oddest is the fitting of a captured American Calliope rocket launcher, which had been removed from a Sherman tank. The 251 series is a popular theme for modellers as there are so many variations not only available as kits, but which can be built by converting existing kits.

Chapter Nine

Lifelong Learning and Sharing

Lots of things have changed over the fifty years or so that I have been modelling and I am happy to say that I am still learning all the time, and loving it. Back in 1985, I first contributed a monthly 'Armoured Column' in *Airfix Magazine* before it closed down later that year. After that, I wrote for *Military Modelling* magazine for thirty-one years and I owe a special thanks to the then editor Ken Jones and later Kelvin Barber for their support over so many years, only giving up at the end of 2016. In 2017, I took on the role of Editor of *Tankette*, the bimonthly magazine for members of MAFVA (*see* below). In all this time, the modelling world has changed a lot. So let's think about magazines for a moment. Like so many paper-based publications these days, sales volumes are a fraction of what they used to be. Personally, and perhaps my age is a significant influence, I like the feel of good-quality paper and the ability to sit and read them as and when I choose, without needing to spend yet more time staring at a computer screen of one sort or another. Sadly, this reduction in sales is common to all paper-based periodicals and if we want them to carry on, we as modellers need to give them our support. While some magazines have come and gone from the market over the years, the hobby still seems healthy.

I know a number of old friends who save storage space by cutting out the articles they are interested in and want to keep, and throwing out the rest. Alternatively, they flick through a magazine in the local newsagent and, depending on the content, decide to buy it or not. Purely my opinion, but one which I have learnt from per-sonal experience, is that over a longer period of time, one's interests change and it is easy to regret having overlooked something in the past that would later be useful. Hence I support the idea of a subscription, which does save money as well, and hanging on to the complete issues. The downside, of course, is having sufficient storage space, but I am grateful that I have a collection of every issue of *Military Modelling* magazine from Issue 1 to the present day, some forty-four years' worth of invaluable information.

MAFVA

Another very valuable resource over the years has been *Tankette*, a publication for members of MAFVA (Model Armoured Fighting Vehicle Association). This is set to begin its fifty-third year of publication. For a great part of that time, it was produced in a small A5 format document, but a few years ago changed to the larger A4 size, which it maintains today. MAFVA is not a commercial operation – it is all about friends with a common interest sharing knowledge and assistance among themselves. In my new role as Editor of *Tankette*, this is not a paid job, but something I have chosen to do to help and encourage others to share our hobby. A key feature of *Tankette*, and one that is intended to continue, is to feature research articles on a variety of topics that you simply can't find anywhere else.

Annual membership of MAFVA is just £16.00 for UK-based members at the moment, which includes receiving *Tankette* six times a year.

Tankette, the bimonthly magazine for members of MAFVA – an old A5 size issue and the current larger A4 magazine.

Overseas membership is more expensive, but that is simply a reflection of the higher cost of posting out the paper copies of *Tankette* to international destinations. Even then, it is cheaper than the cost of a new 1/35 kit and this can be saved if you take advantage of certain traders' discounts for members of MAFVA when shopping with them.

FINALLY …

One of the messages to pass on to any reader/modeller is to encourage you to join in and share your experiences. Even if you are something of a newcomer to the hobby, you can still make a valuable contribution. Just relating what interests you have, what brought you into the hobby and indeed what keeps you going are all helpful, as well as tips about methods or techniques that you find useful. There is not a guarantee that if you submit something to a magazine (who may pay you for the contribution), or to *Tankette* (which doesn't pay contributors as it is not a commercial publication), it will be published, but the editor should consider it and provide feedback. You will need to write something, maybe take some photos, and send them in before any editor can say if it is usable or not. I have had requests on occasions when someone wants a commitment to publish before they take the time to prepare anything. That is not a realistic request, I'm afraid – you need to put something into it first. There is always a chance that it may repeat something that has already been used or submitted, but don't let that stop you trying. If we don't encourage new modellers to submit new material, there remains a danger of being too reliant upon some individuals who may become indisposed for whatever reason.

It is all very well making good use of the information that is shared, but consider what you can contribute in return. I am not one of the world's best modellers, but I started writing when, as a 'customer', I could not find the information I wanted about what was available to me. Since then, I have tried my best to share the knowledge I have gained in an effort to help and encourage others to get the level of enjoyment from the hobby that it has given me. Sharing our experience is vital to the continued vibrancy of our hobby. Don't just sit back and wait for other people to do something, but jump in and share your contributions to encourage others as well.

The other significant change during my modelling lifetime has been the appearance of the Internet. It is unquestionably a great resource. It has really opened up the hobby market to the whole world and tutorials on YouTube can be really helpful for demonstrating various techniques. Equally, if you are looking for a photo of such and such a bit of kit, it is invaluable. I started my first website in the 1990s, then went on to edit the MilitaryModelling.com website for seven years, before starting a new personal site in 2017, at www.militarymodelscene.com, intending just to share my passion for our hobby.

My aim is to encourage you to try your hand at a great hobby and, in the case of German armour of World War II, get what you want out of it. I have always felt, and sometimes heard expressed, that a reader might see a model and be put off by the expertise on display and be discouraged that they can't do it as well, just as others are inspired to try to achieve those same standards. There are lots of tips and techniques to try, especially in the modelling press and thanks to the Internet and YouTube. Have a look at what you find, try them out and decide for yourself if they are for you or not.

Whatever your preference, what I've tried to give you is an idea of the huge range of models that are available for German AFV modellers. Whether you are a dedicated modeller of highly detailed 1/35 models, a collector of small-scale models (they do take up less space), a wargamer or whatever, there is something out there for you. I suspect many, like me, will have started modelling as a youngster, with pocket-money Airfix kits. The continued release of highly detailed 1/35 scale models, some now with interior detail, and even much larger 1/16 models, means these are no longer pocket-money toys. It is the growth of the adult modelling market and a demand for ever more detail from customers who have a disposable income that feeds the development of these more expensive models. I am lucky enough to enjoy these more expensive kits myself, but I don't want to lose sight of the need to encourage youngsters and those who cannot afford the more expensive options to be able to enjoy our hobby with us. Whatever it is you want from this hobby of ours, I wish it will provide you with all the enjoyment that it has me over so many years.

Bibliography

There are hundreds, if not thousands, of books on the market published over the years that cover the topic of German AFVs. It would be impossible to try to list them all and with the new publications coming on stream any list would quickly be out of date. So what I am listing here are some of the ones which I turn to most regularly and have found helpful over the years. Not all are necessarily still in print, but searching on the Internet will usually find them for sale via second-hand book dealers or by individuals, and sometimes at bargain prices, though not always.

Anderson, Thomas, *Panther* (Oxford: Osprey Publishing)

Anderson, Thomas, *Tiger* (Oxford: Osprey Publishing)

Archer, Lee and others, *PanzerWrecks 1–21* (Sussex: PanzerWrecks)

Chamberlain, Peter and Doyle, Hilary L., *Encyclopedia of German AFVs* (London: Arms & Armour Press)

Chamberlain, Peter and Milsom, John, *German Armoured Cars of WW2* (London: Arms & Armour Press)

Culver, Bruce, *Panzer Colours Volumes 1, 2 and 3* (Carrollton, TX: Squadron Signal)

Davis, Brian L., *German Army Uniforms and Insignia 1933–1945* (London: Arms & Armour Press)

Davies, W.J.K., *Wehrmacht Camouflage & Markings 1939–1945* (Almark Publishing)

Ellis, Chris (Editor), *Wheeled Vehicles of the Wehrmacht* (Ducimus: long out of print)

Ellis, Craig, *Panzer IV on the Battlefield* (Keszthely, Hungary: Peko Publishing)

Hartman, Theodor, *Wehrmacht Divisional Signs, 1938–1945* (Almark Publishing)

Ko án, František and Vesely, Alois, *Wireless for Wehrmacht* (Coalville, Leics: WWP Books)

Laugier, Didier, *Sturmartillerie, Vols 1 & 2* (St Martin-des-Entrées: Heimdal [French language])

Lefevre, Eric, *Panzers in Normandy, Then and Now* (Old Harlow, Essex: After the Battle Publications)

Milsom, John, *German Half-Tracked Vehicles of WW2* (London: Arms & Armour Press)

Müller, Peter and Zimmerman, Wolfgang, *Sturmgeschütz III, Vols 1 & 2* (Stockholm, Sweden: History Facts)

Münch, Karlheinz, *Combat History of Schwere Panzerjäger Abteilung 653* (Winnipeg, MB: J.J. Fedorowicz Publishing)

Nafziger, George F., *The German Order of Battle Panzers and Artillery in WW2* (London: Greenhill Books)

Pallud, J.-P. and Ramsey, Winston G., *Battle of the Bulge, Then and Now* (Old Harlow, Essex: After the Battle Publications)

Pallud, J.-P., *Blitzkrieg in the West, Then and Now* (Old Harlow, Essex: After the Battle Publications)

Pallud, J.-P., Ruckmarsch, *The German Retreat from Normandy, Then and Now* (Old Harlow, Essex: After the Battle Publications)

Panczel, Matyas, *Sturmgeschütz III on the Battlefield, Vols 1, 2 & 3* (Keszthely, Hungary: Peko Publishing)

Schneider, Wolfgang, *Tigers in Combat Vols 1, 2 and 3* (Mechanicsburg, PA: Stackpole Publishing)

Stern, Robert C., Greer, Don and Volstad, Ronald, *SS Armour: Pictorial History of the Armoured Formations of the Waffen SS* (Carrollton, TX: Squadron Signal)

Various authors, *Images of War* (A huge series of photos books by various authors and many covering German Panzers; check the Pen and Sword website www.pen-and-sword.co.uk) (Barnsley, Yorkshire: Pen and Sword)

Vollert, Jochen, Pz T34-747(r) as *Beutepanzer in German Service* (Germany: Tankograd)

Williamson, J., Halbkettenfahrzeug, *German Half-Track Vehicles 1939–45* (Almark Publishing)

Windrow, Martin and Embleton, Gerry, *Tank and AFV Crew Uniforms since 1916* (Carrollton, TX: Squadron Signal)

Wise, Terence, *D-Day to Berlin* (Carrollton, TX: Squadron Signal)

Zaloga, Steven J., *Blitzkrieg: Armour Camouflage and Markings 1939–1940* (Carrollton, TX: Squadron Signal)

Zaloga, Steven J. and Grandsen, James, *The Eastern Front: Armour Camouflage and Markings 1941–1945* (Carrollton, TX: Squadron Signal)

Useful Contacts

Kit Manufacturers

Manufacturer	Material	Scales	Notes	Website URL
Academy	Plastic	1/72 1/35		http://academy.co.kr/
Accurate Armour	Resin	1/35		https://accurate-armour.com/
Ace Models	Plastic	1/72	Short-run injection-moulded kits	http://acemodel.com.ua/en
AFV Club	Plastic	1/35		http://en.hobbyfan.com.tw/index-1.asp?language=en
Airfix	Plastic	1/76 1/32		https://www.airfix.com/uk-en/
AlBy Models	Resin	1/72		Available through - http://www.blackliondecals.nl/
Amusing Hobby	Plastic	1/35		http://www.amusinghobby.com/
Attack Hobby Kits	Resin & plastic	1/72		http://attack-kits.eu/
Azimut Production	Resin and plastic kits and conversion	1/72 1/35		http://www.azimutproductions.com/
Bandai	Plastic	1/48	No longer in production	N/A
Black Dog	Resin	1/72 1/48 1/35	Accessories and stowage sets	http://www.blackdog.cz/
Bronco Models	Plastic	1/35		http://www.cn-bronco.com/en/index.php
CMK	Resin	1/72 1/35	Accessories, kits and stowage sets	http://www.cmkkits.com/en/
Den Bels	Resin	1/72		Available through - http://www.blackliondecals.nl/
Des Kit	Resin	1/35		http://deskit.online.fr/
Dragon	Plastic	1/144 1/72 1/35		http://dragon-models.com/
Eduard	Etched accessories and plastic kits	1/72 1/35	Huge range of products	https://www.eduard.com/
First to Fight	Plastic	1/72		http://wrzesien1939.pl/?lang=en
Fujimi	Plastic	1/76	Fujimi also includes the old Nitto kits	http://www.fujimimokei.com/
GHQ	Metal	1/285		http://www.ghqmodels.com/
Giesbers Models	Resin	1/76		Available through - http://www.blackliondecals.nl/
Hasegawa	Plastic	1/72		http://www.hasegawa-model.co.jp/gsite/
Italeri	Plastic	1/72 1/56 1/35	Italeri also now has the old ESCI range	http://www.italeri.com/index.asp
Legend Productions	Resin	1/35		http://www-legend.co.kr/

(continued overleaf)

Manufacturer	Material	Scales	Notes	Website URL
Matador Models	Resin/metal	1/72 1/76	Kits, conversions and accessories	http://matadormodels.co.uk/index.htm
MB Models	Plastic	1/35	Few vehicles plus figures	http://www.mbltd.info/models.htm
Meng	Plastic	1/35		http://www.meng-model.com/
Milicast	Resin	1/76		https://www.milicast.com/
Minitanks	Plastic	1/87		https://www.minitank.net/en/home/index.html
MMS	Metal	1/76	MMS closed in October 2017	http://www.mmsmodels.co.uk/
ModelCollect	Plastic	1/72		http://www.modelcollect.com/
Plastic Soldier Company	Plastic	15mm 20mm	Aimed at wargamers, with multiple kits per box	http://theplasticsoldiercompany.co.uk/
Plus Model	Resin	1/35		http://www.plusmodel.cz/news_en.php
Resicast	Resin	1/35		http://www.resicast.com/
Revell	Plastic	1/72 1/76 1/35	Revell own models are 1/72 plus ex-Matchbox range in 1/76	http://revell.com/
Rye Field Models	Plastic	1/35		Available in the UK via https://www.tigerhobbies.co.uk/
SHQ	Metal	1/72	Large range of vehicles and figures	http://www.shqminiatures.co.uk/
S-Model	Plastic	1/72	Quick assembly, two kits per pack	Available in the UK via http://theplasticsoldiercompany.co.uk/
Takom	Plastic	1/35		http://www.takom-world.com/
Tamiya	Plastic	1/48 1/35		http://www.tamiya.com/
Tiger Models	Plastic	1/72 1/35		http://www.tiger-model.com/
Trident Miniatures	Plastic and resin	1/87		http://www.trident-miniatures.co.at
Trumpeter	Plastic	1/72 1/35 1/16		http://www.trumpeter-china.com/index.php?l=en
UM-MT Models	Plastic	1/72	Originally UM Models but now UM-MT	Available via https://www.hannants.co.uk
Value Gear	Resin	1/72 1/48 1/35	Resin stowage accessories	http://www.valuegeardetails.com/
Voyager Model	Etched-brass, resin, turned- metal barrels	1/72 1/48 1/35		http://voyagermodel.com/
Zvezda	Plastic	1/100 1/72 1/35		http://www.zvezda.org.ru/en/

Paint and Accessory Suppliers

Company	Notes	Website
The Airbrush Company	Distributor for Lifecolor, Alclad II Mil-Spec Paints, Wilder Products, Iwata airbrushes and compressors, Sparmax airbrushes and compressors	https://www.airbrushes.com/
AK Interactive	Paints and weathering products	https://ak-interactive.com/
Ammo of Mig Jiminez	Paints and weathering products	http://www.migjimenez.com/en/
Archer Fine Transfer	Waterslide and dry-rub Transfers	http://www.archertransfers.com/
Deluxe Materials	Glues, diorama accessories etc.	https://www.deluxematerials.co.uk/gb/
Echelon Fine Details	Transfers	http://www.echelonfd.com/
Evergreen Scale Models	Plastic strip, rod, shapes	https://evergreenscalemodels.com/
Hataka	Paints	http://hataka-hobby.com/
Humbrol	Paints	https://www.humbrol.com/uk-en/
JLC Tools	Razor saws and other modellers tools	Available via http://www.modellingtools.co.uk/
Mission Models	Paints	https://www.missionmodelsus.com/
Modelling Tools	Veritable gold mine of useful tools	http://www.modellingtools.co.uk/
Mr Hobby	Paints	http://www.mr-hobby.com/en/
Plastic Soldier Company	Imported to the UK by Tiger Hobbies	http://theplasticsoldiercompany.co.uk/
Revell	Paints	http://revell.com/
Slaters	Plastic card, strip, rod etc.	https://slatersplastikard.com/
Star Decals	Transfers	http://star-decals.net/index.html
Tamiya	Paints, tools	http://www.tamiya.com/
Trumpeter	Tools	http://www.trumpeter-china.com/
Vallejo	Paints	http://www.acrylicosvallejo.com/
Xtracolour	Paints	https://www.hannants.co.uk/manufacturer/xtracolor
Xuron Cutters	Tools	https://www.xuron.com/

Index